# HUMANITIES PROGRAMMING

## A How-To-Do-It Manual

Rhea Joyce Rubin

**HOW-TO-DO-IT MANUALS
FOR LIBRARIANS**

**NUMBER 72**

NEAL-SCHUMAN PUBLISHERS, INC.
New York, London

Published by Neal-Schuman Publishers, Inc.
100 Varick Street
New York, NY 10013

Printed and bound in the United States of America.

**Library of Congress Cataloging-in-Publication Data**

Rubin, Rhea Joyce.
   Humanities programming : a how-to-do-it manual for librarians / Rhea
Joyce Rubin.
      p.   cm.
   Includes bibliographical references and index.
   ISBN 1-55570-083-7
   1. Public libraries—Cultural programs—United States.  2. Humanities—
Study and teaching (Continuing education)—United States.  I. Title.
Z716.R77   1997
021.2'6'0973—dc21                                          96-29838

*To my Honey Bee, Sweet Sixteen*

# CONTENTS

# ACKNOWLEDGMENTS

Nearly fifteen years ago, Tom Phelps and Peggy O'Donnell had the idea to write a book which would assist librarians in getting grants from the National Endowment for the Humanities and in producing humanities programs. Because their proposed project never came to fruition, I have written this book. My thanks to both of them for their encouragement in this endeavor.

I am grateful to the many librarians and others who answered my survey and flooded my office with samples of their wonderful programs. Special thanks to Deb Robertson and Susan Brandehoff of ALA for sharing so many of their files with me. And to Deb and Frannie Ashburn for identifying programming experts to poll and for sharing their program secrets. Deb is a walking "Who's Who" of the field and Frannie is unmatched in both her talent for humorous survey answers and correspondence, and her curiosity about position descriptions and related matters.

As usual, I have written this book in California, alone but not unaided. Two organizations have been invaluable. Schmoop! Enterprises has been my biggest source of office help and UMM Associates has provided much computer assistance. I would like to acknowledge their directors, board members, and employees. CGD has continued to provide security (and other) services.

Finally, my publisher and I are grateful to the planning guru and crossword addict from Massachusetts who forced me to edit the final draft of this manuscripts while verandah-sitting during the second week of May.

# FOREWORD
## BY THOMAS PHELPS

A saying long attributed to Thomas Jefferson, and quoted in the *National Foundation on the Arts and Humanities Act of 1965*, sums up one of the many reasons for the publication of this book. The excerpt is this: *Democracy demands wisdom and vision in its citizens.* This short mot explains in a very few words why libraries, especially public libraries, play a tremendously important role in a democratic society. Libraries hold the key to *wisdom* and *vision* for many citizens nationwide. According to Charles Frankel, who died tragically in 1979, and who was Old Dominion Professor of Philosophy and Public Affairs at Columbia University in New York City, "A public library is, quite simply, a place where there is knowledge. It is the job of the public librarian to diffuse that knowledge among the citizenry of the communities in which they exist." The book you are about to read offers a means by which librarians can perform such a Herculean task.

In 1978 a group of invited participants assembled at the University of North Carolina to discuss "the role of the humanities in the public library." Of particular interest to readers of this book might be one of the questions that emerged from that conference. In a publication resulting from the conference, Lester Asheim, then the William Rand Kenan, Jr. Professor of Library Science at UNC Chapel Hill, asked how public librarians could bring to the citizens of their respective communities the knowledge that occupies the frontiers of scholarship in the humanities (Broadust).

One answer to that question is, of course, to provide the citizens with access to an excellent collection of materials. But is this provision enough? There is little doubt that librarians must be responsible for assembling a useful and meaningful collection of materials, but such collections are of little value if they sit upon the library's shelves. In order that citizens glean *wisdom* and *vision* from these vast, assembled collections, librarians must encourage their use and their interpretation. It is not enough to select and organize materials, librarians must as well aid in an educational enterprise that promotes understanding. The way to do this is to give as many community members as possible the chance to experience the quality of the collections and the quantity of knowledge kept in libraries across this land.

*Wisdom* and *Vision* come in all kinds of packages—not the least of which are books, films, tapes, journals, periodicals, and all other manner of items held in libraries. The essential key is the examination and interpretation of what is inside these wrappers. Librarians can provide an array of opportunities for their citizenry to examine and interpret materials by following the recipes provided in this, Rhea Rubin's *Humanities Programming.* Programmatic activities give ordinary citizens the opportunity to share experiences, emotions, and ideas with those who have already studied and with others who want to learn. It is clear that from such sharing new ideas emerge. And it is more clear that ideas make a positive difference in the lives of people.

Ever since the conference in 1978 mentioned above, the National Endowment for the Humanities has provided support for educational programs in public libraries. Such programs were meant to "enrich individual lives, enhance the common good, and promote effective citizenship by enabling Americans to assess ideas and values." For more than a decade, the NEH has sought to encourage the educational role of cultural institutions and organizations in this country. Reasons for offering support for educational programs in this nation's cultural institutions rests on three assumptions: "(1) that the humanities transmit profound reflections about human life that have shaped our heritage; (2) that the study of the humanities can enrich the lives of all citizens; and (3) that the humanities can be presented effectively to the public without diminishing intellectual substance." (National Endowment) (See: *Guidelines and Application Instructions, Humanities Projects in Libraries and Archives*: National Endowment for the Humanities, 1995) Questions raised by the humanities are universal questions that touch everyone. Fundamental questions addressed by the humanities are central to the thoughts of every man and woman. There is none so unlettered as to escape them; none so learned as to rise above them.

The National Endowment for the Humanities has long believed that public libraries, beyond their intrinsic importance as repositories of vital resources, offer an open setting for community members to gather and discuss fundamental human questions. The NEH also knows that librarians crate educational programs at settings and sites other than the library that reach deep into the communities they serve and extend to diverse community groups. For the past two decades, with major grants, the Endowment has encouraged librarians to present public programs in the humanities. Over such a period of time, many programs employing many formats have been supported and conducted in libraries in every state, district, and territory. Both the Endowment and librarians have assessed these programs and have determined from these assessments "what works" and "what doesn't work." Many people were involved in the creation of these programs, and many were involved in the assessment of them. The author of this book, Rhea Rubin, has been a primary player in both the creation and the assessment of humanities programs in libraries and archives. For example, in 1982, the Endowment made an extensive grant to the American Library Association to design and conduct reading and discussion programs at more than sixty public libraries throughout the nation. During the development stage of the project, it was determined that librarians and scholars in the humanities would need training and constructive assistance in order to effectively promote, conduct, and evaluate programs in their libraries. Rhea Rubin was recruited to write the training manuals and to conduct portions of the training. Much of what Rhea designed then is still used today, some fourteen years later.

Over the past decade, Rhea has refined her designs and her teaching methods, and she has incorporated all of her new-found knowledge into the book you are about to read. She has used astute judgment in her selection of examples of public programs in the humanities at libraries as illustrations in her text. Moreover, she has performed all duties and functions in every aspect of public programming, and she has served many times as a panelist and advisor to the NEH. I believe her book will be a useful tool for librarians who plan to conduct educational programs of any kind for their community members. I am pleased that the results of a national poll indicate that in the opinion of the public, the most important roles for the public library are to support the educational aspirations of the community. These findings suggest that librarians, with the assistance provided by this book, can design, promote, and conduct educational programs in their libraries and thereby inspire *wisdom* and *vision* in their citizens, thereby helping to fulfill the *Jeffersonian dream.*

Thomas C. Phelps
Humanities Projects in Libraries and Archives
Division of Public Programs
National Endowment for the Humanities

# PREFACE

Nineteen ninety-five was the thirtieth anniversary of the National Endowment for the Humanities (NEH), our federal agency devoted to research, education, and public programs in the humanities for people throughout America. For me, 1995 was the twentieth anniversary of my work in the humanities as a public librarian.

As I write *Humanities Programming: A How-to-Do-It Manual for Librarians* I am struck by the irony of both these anniversaries coinciding with congressional debate over the possible closure of the NEH. A 38 percent cut in the 1996 NEH budget is called for in the US Senate-House Appropriations Conference Committee agreement which is most likely to be ratified. This has necessitated a major reorganization at NEH with a 33 percent cut in staff. State humanities councils, which rely on the NEH for 80 percent of their support, are also reconsidering their prospects.

Because of the uncertainty over the future form and funding of NEH and its affiliates, this book cannot contain specifics on their activities or grant programs. The current state of suspense only heightens the need for a rededication of libraries to their endeavors in the humanities. As James Quay and James Veninga stated in their keynote address at the 1989 Wingspread Conference of the National Taskforce on Scholarship and the Public Humanities, "so long as there is the human future, the humanities will be a part of it, for both the subject and the audience of the humanities must endure as long as humans endure" (Quay and Veninga, p. 1).

Libraries agree. Many of them began humanities-based programs under NEH funding, but extended them without additional grants and plan to continue to do so.

The text is based on the experiences of real libraries providing humanities programs. A simple survey was sent to eighty programs in August 1995; fifty-three responded to share their knowledge of over 160 programs. In addition, I queried all of the major national and regional programs. I have interwoven throughout the book quotes from these responses. Now I invite you to listen in on the answers.

This book is divided into seven parts. The first is an introduction to the humanities and to humanities-based programs in libraries. The second part is devoted to planning, from pre-planning through selecting scholars and discussion leaders. Included are worksheets and checklists for both homegrown and pre-designed program series. Parts three through five focus on other aspects of planning: budgeting and funding, building an audience, program management, and evaluation. Although real-life examples from library programs are given throughout the book, parts six and seven describe in detail a number of model programs. The book ends with appendices listing reading and discussion resources, exhibit sources, State Humanities Councils, State Centers for the Book, a bibliography, and an index.

I hope that this step-by-step guide to Humanities Programming will shed light on the excellent program examples around the country, and will inspire you and your library to share the humanities with your communities.

Loudoun Public Libraries Presents

Breaking the
Sound Barrier:
The Literature of
Deafness

Authors &
Illustrators

Ticket

God, Evil,
and the
Literary
Imagination

TAR HEEL
FICTION:
Literary Perspectives
on North Carolina

Let's Talk About It
Reading and Discussion
Programs in America's
Libraries

Reynolds Price, Thomas Wolfe, Doris Betts, Charles Chesnutt, John Ehle

ussion
raries

nities

**LIVING TOGETHER
BY SCOTT SANDERS**

The Ohio Humanities
Council has adopted
"Community
Reconsidered" as a
theme in response to
growing public interest in
how we shape and define
the places where
we live. The Council
invites you to take part in
book discussions at
public libraries across
Ohio. Join friends,
neighbors, and
humanities scholars to
explore the meaning of
community, past and
present.

In "Living Together,"
author Scott Sanders
asks a tough question
facing most Americans —
"What do we make of the
struggle between the self
and community?" The
stories he has chosen for
this book discussion
program urge readers to
consider the role of
community life in shaping
the individual.

"Except for the rare
hermit, we all live in
communities. We depend
on other people, near and
far, for most of our daily
needs, for companionship,
for care. We depend on
families for love, on
neighbors for help, on
strangers for hospitals
and roads. Without the
work of many hands and
heads, there would be
no food on our tables,
no tools between us and
the rain, no books to
read or music to hear or
clothes to wear. Our
very language, our
values and ideas, our
notions of what it
means to be human,
arise from the life we
share with others."

Scott Sanders

**COMMUNITY RECONSIDERED**

# 1 INTRODUCTION

---

## WHAT ARE THE HUMANITIES AND WHY ARE THEY IMPORTANT?

"The humanities explore what it means to be human. Through history, literature, and philosophy, we engage in our most vital inheritance: the wisdom of our cultures, the experience of remarkable people, and the values that define and guide our lives as persons and as a people. The humanities invite us to lifelong learning, to continuing conversation about what matters to each and all of us" (California Council for the Humanities, p. 25). A piece of the California Council for the Humanities vision statement, this quote reflects my own thinking on the substance and importance of the humanities.

The humanities are commonly defined by the many and disparate academic disciplines implied. But a shared goal joins them: the search to understand the infinite mysteries of human existence. The humanities are the branches of learning that deal with what people have felt and believed, with what humans consider important and valuable. Usually "humanities" refers to all subjects of study that are outside those of science (bodies of knowledge) or creative arts (music, dance, theater, painting, sculpture, or literature). The humanities differ from the arts, which focus on a product and on creative skills. The humanities differ from the sciences, which concentrate on measuring and describing an environment so that it might be changed. The humanities includes the discussion, criticism, and history of knowledge and aptitude, but not the discipline of science or the creation of works of art. For example, doing a physics experiment is not the stuff of humanities, but debating the value of public funding of science experimentation is. Painting a portrait is not humanities, but discussing the role of portrait painting in the nineteenth century is.

Charles Frankel, a teacher and statesman committed to scholarship and public affairs, described the humanities as a society's "efforts to place itself in the sequence of history, to examine its ideas and ideals, to study its language and its forms of behavior, to come to a critical assessment of the myths, symbols, stories, rules, by which it gives shape and direction to its life. And they are something more—they are its efforts to look beyond its own parochial frontiers, and to see itself against the much larger background of the human drama at large and all the varieties of human nature and experience" (Frankel, pp. 80–81).

To be more specific, the legislation which established the National Endowment for the Humanities utilizes this definition: "The term 'humanities' includes, but is not limited to, the study of the following: language, both modern and classical; linguistics; literature; history; jurisprudence; philosophy; archaeology; comparative religion; ethics; the history, criticism, and theory of the arts; those aspects of the social sciences which have humanistic content and employ humanistic methods; and the study and application of the humanities to the human environment with particular attention to reflecting our diverse heritage, traditions, and history and to the relevance of the humanities to the current conditions of everyday life" (National Endowment for the Humanities, 1995, p. 1).

The National Foundation on the Arts and the Humanities Act 1965 begins with the statement "Democracy demands wisdom and vision in its citizens." The NEH was called upon to encourage inquiry and achievement in "the realm of ideas and of the spirit" (National Endowment for the Humanities, 1995, p. 1).

The National Endowment for the Humanities encourages three types of programs.

1. The appreciation and interpretation of cultural works. This includes involving the public in historical, critical, or theoretical approaches to literature, music, theater, and art.
2. The illumination of historical ideas, figures, and events. The NEH encourages reflective and analytical treatment of historical events, figures, and movements.
3. An understanding of the disciplines of the humanities. This refers to programs which provide the public with an awareness of the methods and the insights of any humanities discipline.

Robert Benedetti, Dean of the College, University of the Pacific, has written: "The humanities . . . focus our personal meditations and fulfill our private needs. They exercise the mind and help us find meaning within the humdrum of life . . . But the humanities promise public as well as private rewards. Republics throughout history have urged citizens to reflect upon their cultural heritage. Cicero encouraged every Roman to master the liberal arts . . . Jefferson expected all citizens to know the humanities, founding a university to provide them access. However, our generation has lost confidence in cultural reflection . . . " He explains

"The humanities let us learn about ourselves and our history, but perhaps even more importantly, the humanities foster human contact." Sheldon Hackney

"I know of no safe depository for the ultimate powers of society than the people themselves. And, if we think them not enlightened enough to exercise their control with a wholesome discretion, the remedy is not to take it from them, but to inform their discretion." Thomas Jefferson

the current policy focus on technological advances which leads to priority status for the sciences but stresses that the humanities still have a place in every citizen's education. "First, while science deals with the means available to reach our goals, it does not uncover what those goals should be. To create communities and to move them forward, we need to discover common commitments . . . Secondly, values grow out of individual experience. We often lack words to articulate feelings. The humanities provide linguistic strategies to communicate what we hold dear and would preserve. In other words, the humanities not only focus attention on values, but provide a vocabulary for sharing them . . . Finally, the search for values and the language to express them can lead to prejudice and intolerance. Fascism followed in the wake of nineteenth century Romanticism, a treasure trove of humanistic tendencies. However, the humanities also provide antidotes for these tendencies. They not only help us define our own universe, but also introduce us to other 'universes.' They teach empathy, offer alternative 'structure of feeling,' and search for universals . . . If we are to reestablish a life together, we must enrich our understanding of ourselves, learn to communicate what we believe, and appreciate beliefs which are different from our own" (Benedetti, pp. 1–6).

"88% of Americans feel that the humanities help bring people together." National Cultural Alliance study, 1993.

America's citizens agree with Benedetti. According to a 1993 survey commissioned by the National Cultural Alliance, Americans greatly value the arts and humanities. A vast majority agreed that the arts and humanities "help people learn about those of different cultural and ethnic groups" (91%) and "help bring people together" (88%). 77% agreed with the statement "The arts and humanities provide an anchor or reference point in a world of turmoil." Nearly a third (31%) of respondents view the arts and humanities as playing a "major role" in their lives, and another 57% say they play a "minor role" (National Cultural Alliance, pp. 2–8).

## WHY HUMANITIES PROGRAMS IN LIBRARIES?

The humanities demand our attention so that we can:

- understand our mutual human heritage
- derive meaning from our experiences

- make connections between our own times and others, our own lives and others
- explore multiple points of view

Libraries are the ideal place for such investigations because they:

- are one of the few places accessible to all at no charge
- serve no special interests but belong to all
- have a wealth of print and non-print resources
- are seen as neutral and non-threatening

Now, more than ever, libraries must reassert their claim to "territory in the life of the mind" so that commercial venues, such as chain bookstores, do not become the only centers for cultural and intellectual programs. The library has an historic obligation to provide intellectual stimulation, support for independent learning and development, and cultural activities.

The idea of actively promoting, presenting, and interpreting the library's collection through programming dates back to the nineteenth century. Both public and popular libraries have offered programs for the past two hundred years. Popular libraries of the nineteenth and early twentieth century included subscription-based popular reading libraries, membership athenaeums, and philanthropist-funded trade-related libraries. All hosted non-book activities to attract members and to entice audiences for their "moral improvement." These activities, carried out with a missionary zeal, ranged from lectures and debates to musical concerts and art exhibits to balls and soirees.

With the demise of privately funded libraries, the new public libraries carried on the tradition of educational and cultural programming. The original stated reasons were to:

- increase circulation
- promote reading and the use of books
- provide a moral and spiritual uplift through arts and culture
- encourage the use of libraries as social and recreation centers

Traditionally the public library has been the source of education and recreation for the out-of-school adult. The public library was heavily involved in the adult education movements of the 1930s and 1940s. In librarianship, adult education stemmed from reading guidance but differentiated itself by emphasizing group work and formalized programming. Adult education, according to Margaret E. Monroe, had "an emphasis on purposeful reading, a stress on the library's materials as sources of ideas to be put to use, and a fulfillment of the [library's] commitment to a democratic society" (Monroe, 1963, p. 2). As a center for adult independent learning, the library supplied resources for self-education and supplemented this education with personalized reading lists and curricula, tutorials, and humanities programs such as book discussions and lecture series.

The first documented library discussion programs were held by the New York Public Library in 1927 using an American Library Association (ALA) bibliography entitled "Classics of the Western World." The Great Books discussion series, founded at the University of Chicago in 1945, was another predecessor of today's humanities programs. In 1948 the ALA developed a national discussion program, "Great Issues," and in 1951 the ALA sponsored the American Heritage Project with the Fund for Adult Education.

In the 1970s the National Endowment for the Humanities (NEH) began to fund humanities programs in public library programs. Although originally NEH programs were almost exclusively held on college campuses, many out-of-school adults felt uncomfortable in the academic world. The public library was again the preferred alternative because of its informal, non-threatening atmosphere and for its humanities collections in print and non-print. As Lynne Cheney put it in her 1988 report on the NEH, "Public programming in the humanities is now so substantive and extensive that it has become a kind of parallel school, one that has grown up outside the established institutions of education" (Cheney, p. 27).

Many public libraries have been slow to adopt adult programming despite their commitment to programs for children. The libraries which do offer programs suggest the following reasons:

- increase the visibility of the library and community awareness of library resources
- provide information and education in a variety of ways to meet differing learning styles as well as diverse educational needs
- offer an alternative to commercial entertainment
- make the library vital for users of non-books as well as print readers
- demonstrate viability to government leaders, taxpayers, and funding agencies
- increase circulation
- provide a public forum for the exchange of ideas
- develop cooperation with other community agencies and organizations

- engage diverse participants
- expand the library's sphere of influence

The need for public programs in the library is greater than ever. Now that money is tight, leisure time is increasing, literacy is decreasing, and life expectancy is lengthening, the library is being called upon to provide educational and cultural opportunities. Humanities programs are only one aspect of this picture, but an essential one.

Much has been made of late twentieth century America as an information society. But studies show that libraries are not often looked at as sources of information and, even when they are, that the interpretation and analysis of information is still lacking. Quay and Veninga state that "we all know where the public tends to get its information: broadcast media, mostly television, followed by newspapers and magazines. There may be other sources of information – one's co-workers, friends, parents. But where do Americans get their *knowledge*? Where do they find knowledge that integrates information into broader contexts of value, time, and place . . . " (Quay and Veninga, p. 11). Both the humanities and the library are key answers.

Librarians naturally agree with Barbara Tuchman, the historian, who wrote "Without books, history is silent, literature dumb, science crippled, thought and speculation at a standstill. Without books, the development of civilization would have been impossible. They are engines of change, windows on the world, and lighthouses erected in the sea of time. They are companions, teachers, magicians, bankers of the treasures of the mind. Books are humanity in print" (Tuchman, p. 1). And programs—of all kinds—are what bring the books to life through analysis and interpretation.

Linda Holtslander of the Loudon Public Libraries writes: "The libraries are an incredible resource for the community. Bringing real artists, real authors, real *people* into the library is so important. With all of today's technology, we forget that people are still writing books, people are still painting, making music, approaching life directly—not through a computer screen . . . Everyone benefits [from programs]—the community responses are very positive, scholars and artists recognize that they are reaching new audiences, and the libraries are drawing more people, in many cases parts of the community we don't normally see . . . "*

---

*Quotes such as these come out of my 1995 Survey (see p. xiii for more information on the survey).

Libraries which hesitate to provide programs often underestimate all of the above and cite lack of staff time and funding as major impediments. This book is designed to provide the tools to embark on humanities programs without fear.

On a more personal level, humanities programs are fun and rewarding for staff. As Frannie Ashburn, the director of the North Carolina Center for the Book, says humanities programming is "life-altering and mind-bending work for programmers and participants. It's work you can actually *enjoy*. It's education at its very best, lifelong learning in the user-friendly atmosphere of your public library. Just good reading, good conversation, and the opportunity to learn about life (your own and the characters in the books and the characters in the discussion group). And it's *fun*."

# 2 PLANNING

Four elements are fundamental: Enthusiasm and energy; administrative support; funding; and time.

There are four fundamental elements for successful humanities programming:

- You must believe in the value of humanities programs and that they can work in your library. Your enthusiasm and energy are vital.
- You must have the support of your administration, board, and staff.
- You will need money to cover the program's expenses. Although budgeting and funding are covered in Chapter 3, you need to keep finances in mind as you plan; many choices can hinge on the level of funding available.
- You must allow enough time to plan carefully. As one respondent stated: "A first effort should include over-preparation. Talk through the process with an experienced coordinator . . . " This chapter is an attempt to replace that face to face chat by bringing you many experienced programmers' suggestions.

According to the librarians who responded to my survey on humanities programming, planning is key. All have had experience with library programs and, though they differ on which parts of planning are more or less fun, difficult, or time-consuming, they all agree that good preparation is the cornerstone of success.

Here are six clusters of questions you should ask yourself before planning a program. Your answers will clarify whether you are ready and able to plan and present a humanities program while pointing you toward the areas which will need most of your attention.

1. *Priorities*. What are your library's goals and objectives? Whom are you trying to reach? What is your philosophy of service?
2. *Present Services*. What is your library offering now? Would humanities programming enhance these services? Would they fit into an existing program?
3. *Resources*. What is the present staff work load? Is there time to devote to a new service? If not, are there special funds to hire people to assist staff? Are there creative skills among staff members which are underused? Do you have a special collection that could be promoted through humanities programs?

4. *Commitment.* Is the library administration and board supportive of this kind of endeavor? Are other staff members interested? Are there community agencies that could be natural and cooperative partners? Are there other libraries which might co-sponsor a program series?

5. *Community.* Is there an audience for exploring the humanities? Are there other cultural institutions providing this kind of activity? If so, might the library collaborate on it instead of doing its own? What impacts on the community do you anticipate resulting from humanities programs? What might result for the library?

6. *Goal.* What purpose(s) do you have for providing humanities programs in the library? What are your optimal goals?

If you cannot answer all of these questions off the cuff, preplanning is a good idea. As its name suggests, pre-planning precedes the detailed planning of an actual program. Sometimes called "planning to plan," this process assesses the library's probability for success by identifying key players, possible obstacles, and necessary strategies. Following is a pre-planning worksheet to help you.

# PRE-PLANNING WORKSHEET

**BENEFIT ANALYSIS:**

1.  What are my goals for producing a humanities program?

    _____
    _____
    _____

2.  How will the program benefit my library?

    _____
    _____
    _____

3.  How will the program augment (or conflict with) the library's stated goals?

    _____
    _____
    _____

4.  How will the program benefit the participants? The greater community?

    _____
    _____
    _____

**OBSTACLES**

1.  What potential obstacles are you aware of?

    _____
    _____
    _____

2.  Who has the power to remove or minimize these obstacles?

    _____
    _____
    _____

3.  How can you enlist her/his assistance?

    _____
    _____
    _____

## COMMITMENT

1. Can you get a commitment of support from your supervisor? From her/his supervisor? Library Director? Board member(s)?

   _____
   _____
   _____

2. How can you enlist their commitment?

   _____
   _____
   _____

## COMMUNITY PORTRAIT

1. What do you know about the community's interest in the humanities? In cultural or intellectual programs? (For example, is there a local arts council that has done a study or made a report? Is there a local college or university which has done field research?)

   _____
   _____
   _____

2. What are the community's demographics? (For example, age ranges and changes in them; languages spoken; educational level?)

   _____
   _____
   _____

3. What issues are currently facing the community that could form the basis for a program series or create an interest in it? (For example, what are the hot topics in the local papers?)

   _____
   _____
   _____

4. Is there a special aspect of the community which could be highlighted in a program? (For example, is it an anniversary year in the town's history? Are the newest immigrants a different ethnicity?)

   _____
   _____
   _____

## LIBRARY RESOURCES

1. *Collection*: Will the general humanities collection support the programming? Will it need to be expanded (through purchase or loan) to support the program? Are there special collections (e.g. local history) which could relate to humanities programming? Are there AV materials (e.g. films, photos) that can be used?

   _____

   _____

   _____

2. *Facilities and Equipment*: Does the library have suitable and accessible meeting rooms? Does the library own AV equipment? Does the library have other equipment which may be necessary (e.g. microphone or assistive listening system)?

   _____

   _____

   _____

3. *Staff Expertise*: Does the library have staff members with experience in programming? In humanities content? In public relations? In working with scholars? In writing grant proposals? In fund raising?

   _____

   _____

   _____

4. *Staff Time:* How much staff time is presently devoted to develop programs? How much staff time is available? Could additional staff be assigned? Who has the power to do this?

   _____

   _____

   _____

## COMMUNITY RESOURCES

1. *Cultural Institutions:* Are there other cultural institutions in the area providing such programs? If so, might the library collaborate? Might they cooperate on the library's endeavor (e.g. mount an exhibit relating to the topic)?

   _____

   _____

2. *Community Agencies:* Are there other agencies or organizations which might be natural and cooperative partners?

_____
_____
_____

3. *Planning Committee Members:* Are there individuals with particular interest or expertise who might serve on a planning committee?

_____
_____
_____

4. *Resource People:* Are there individuals (or organizations) which might be willing to help with implementation (e.g. fund raising or publicity)?

_____
_____
_____

5. *Scholars:* Are there scholars who might assist in the planning or implementation?

_____
_____
_____

6. *Discussion Group Leaders:* Are there individuals with experience in leading group discussions?

_____
_____
_____

7. *Facilities:* If the library lacks space, are there other facilities available in the community? Equipment for loan?

_____
_____
_____

8. *Media:* What media are available to provide publicity? (For example, local papers, shoppers' papers, community newsletters, radio and TV?)

_____
_____
_____

9. *Collections*: Are there special collections of books or AV materials in local agencies or organizations? Are they accessible?

_____

_____

_____

## FUNDING

1. *In-House Budget:* Is there a line in the budget for adult programs? If not, can funds be transferred from other lines? Who has the power to do this?

_____

_____

_____

2. *Special Library Funding:* Is funding available from the Friends of the Library? The library foundation? An endowment?

_____

_____

_____

3. *Community Funding:* Is funding available from local organizations? Foundations?

_____

_____

_____

4. *Commercial Sponsorship:* Is there a local business which might sponsor the programs and provide funds and/or in-kind contributions? For example, a bookstore or an art store?

_____

_____

_____

5. *Grants:* Is there staff or volunteer time available to write grant proposals? Does the library have any expertise in this area?

_____

_____

_____

## STAFF AND ADMINISTRATIVE COMMITMENT

After you have completed the pre-planning worksheets, it is time to talk to other library staff members and administrators. It is essential to have the support of both. Your answers on the pre-planning worksheet provide you with the "ammunition" to win their backing. Since you have thought through both benefits and potential obstacles, you are prepared to answer questions and entice their commitment. Perhaps you will want to present your idea at a staff meeting to test reactions. Many program planners have been happily surprised by the enthusiasm greeted a new project which is perceived as "fun" and "beneficial to the library and community."

But sometimes fellow staff members will be disinterested or antagonistic. Even if staff are not interested in *planning* the program, your request for their participation is important to defuse potential hostility. By keeping them informed of the planning process and requesting their input, you may be ensuring their cooperation later in the implementation stage. Remember that even if they are not actively involved, any new venture in the library impacts the whole staff by increasing public questions and book circulation in certain areas and by affecting staff scheduling.

If the administration is disinterested, it is crucial that you find that out early on. One way to elicit support is to relate the program's objectives to goals which the administration already endorses. A caveat: It is almost impossible to plan and present a program without administrative support. Partner agencies, funding sources, advisory committees will all expect the library director or her/his representative to demonstrate support before they will work with you.

## PROGRAM COORDINATOR

The program coordinator has the major responsibility for all parts of planning and implementing the program series. Many tasks can be delegated to others, such as the planning committee members, scholar, and discussion leaders, but the coordinator must supervise the entire project.

So far it has been assumed that you, the reader, will be the

"Remain forever curious."

program coordinator. If so, heed this advice from J. Ingrid Lesley of the Chicago Public Library: "Be a reader. Love gallery and museum visiting—take in exhibits. Remain forever curious, a characteristic which can keep you energetic, young, and contemporary. Read—even if several days late—a good newspaper to keep abreast of many things."

If you are not to be the coordinator, who is? In most cases, the coordinator is a librarian. In small libraries, the coordinator is usually the director while in medium-sized libraries, an administrator or a public services librarian often is recruited.

Sometimes the librarian is temporarily excused from regular duties—which are handled by a paid substitute—to run the program. In large libraries, there may be a position responsible for lifelong learning, for programs, or for community development, and this person is the coordinator. Only a few public libraries such as Howard County Library (MD), Monroe County Library System (MI), Loudon Public Libraries (VA), Greenville County Library (SC), and Prince George's County Memorial Library System (MD) have full-time programming staff (either one full-time position or two positions each with half-time devoted to programs).

In some cases, whatever size the library, the coordinator is not a librarian but a humanist on the staff of another agency or an experienced programmer (humanist or librarian) hired by the library on a temporary basis to spearhead the program. There are also a few freelancers serving as project directors for humanities programs on a contractual basis.

The single most important person in the creation and implementation of a successful program series is the coordinator, so s/he must be selected carefully. Based on an examination of many popular programs, six qualities seem to be the most significant:

- Enthusiasm and the ability to transmit it to others
- Capacity and willingness to work productively with the community
- Good communication skills (i.e. writing, consulting, speaking)
- Creativity and the ability to bring innovative concepts to the fore
- Administrative abilities including time management, attention to detail, and the ability to make decisions
- People skills to coordinate the committee members, scholars, discussion leaders, and library staff

Even a person with all the wonderful qualities listed above needs something else: the time to devote to the project. Again, hiring temporary assistance (e.g. clerical help, a publicity consultant) should be considered.

Ideally, the coordinator should be selected (or hired) before planning goes any further so that his/her skills are fully utilized. If it is necessary to select him/her after a committee is convened, use the committee members to help locate and interview potential coordinators. If it is necessary to select the coordinator after theme development, turn that to your advantage by looking for someone with special interest or knowledge in the topic.

## JOB DESCRIPTION: PROGRAM COORDINATOR

*Responsibilities:*
- Selection of planning committee members
- Facilitation of theme development and materials selection
- Selection and coordination of scholars
- Selection and coordination of discussion leaders, if needed
- Coordination of assisting staff or volunteers
- Delegation of responsibilities to committee members
- Distribution of materials
- Preparation of budget
- Development of publicity
- Management of each program, including preparation of meeting room, supplies, and equipment; introduction of program, scholar, and discussion leaders; wrap-up of program
- Payment of honoraria and other bills
- Reports as required
- Evaluation

# PLANNING COMMITTEE

Now you are ready to select a planning committee. A well-chosen group of five to eight people can be invaluable for their contributions of ideas, their actual labor in planning and implementation, and their contacts in the community which can lead to funding and other resources and to potential audiences.

This committee should be a decision-making body with well-defined responsibilities. Among these are:

- To discuss—and revise if necessary—goals that you have developed
- To define the audience
- To help reach that audience
- To determine the theme or topic of the program(s)
- To suggest organizations and individuals with knowledge in the topic area who would be helpful in building the program
- To help select scholars (and discussion leaders if needed)

In selecting committee members, try to include one or more of each of these:

- Trustees or Friends of the library who can assist with commitment and contacts
- Community members with an interest in the humanities who can generate enthusiasm and help build an audience
- Local business owners and others who can assist with securing local support and/or funding
- Staff of other agencies which can produce exhibits to complement the theme, provide AV assistance, or contribute other expertise and resources
- People with publicity skills and/or media contacts
- Scholars who can assist in the selection of topics, materials, and speakers
- Library staff members

## COMMUNITY COLLABORATION

"Think holistically."

Although the last section recommended that the planning committee include staff of other community agencies, local business owners, and residents of your area, the planning committee is only one venue for collaboration. To increase the participation in—and the longevity of—your program, collaboration at each stage of planning is essential. Mary Treacy of the Minnesota Center for the Book writes "Recognize what the library/librarian can do well and what others can do better. Think holistically, not just about the program but about all the many facets that can support, give longer life to, enhance, and enrich the single event."

Cooperation may breed programs the library alone would not have thought of, or could not do in isolation.

First, cooperation may breed simple, locally-based programs the library alone would not have thought of, or could not do in isolation. Wanda Gardner of the Decorah (IA) Public Library reminds us "Think of the tie-ins you can make to a local event. When our local college had a production of Ibsen's 'A Doll's House,' we purchased copies of the play and had a discussion before the performance. As a community with Norwegian roots, we invited local history students who had just read the play in Norwegian, and exhibited a Victorian dolls house from the Norwegian-American Museum. Great fun! And good public relations."

Second, collaborative planning and implementation speak to the role of the library as central in—and knowledgeable about—the community. As the primary resource for local information, the library knows (better than anyone else in town) who is working on what and with whom. The library answers reference questions from the other agencies and organizations and refers patrons to them as needs require. The library is acting upon its information—and modeling resource sharing—by acting in cooperation with others. By coordinating the development of a humanities program, the library even moves beyond its information sharing role to a leadership position in the community.

> Collaborative planning and implementation speak to the role of the library as central in – and knowledgeable about – the community.

Third, cooperation is a practical response to the growing difficulty of obtaining unilateral funding. The library needs partner agencies and organizations to assist with:

> Cooperation is a practical response to the growing difficulty of finding unilateral funding.

- *Staff time.* Often, staff tasks can be split between two agencies. Each organization provides partial staff support and obtains a total program.
- *Operating costs.* Though most agencies will not make cash contributions to a library program, their inclusion in the program's planning and implementation may result in a sharing of expenses. For example, each agency might take a turn providing postage or refreshments. Sometimes, another agency can make an in-kind contribution of something it owns (e.g. public address system or van) which further reduces the library's cash outlay.
- *Expertise.* Another agency in town may know more than you do about a humanities topic (e.g. the History Society on local history) or about a particular audience (e.g. the VFW about enticing older men to programs) or about a resource (e.g. the community college about local poets).
- *Facility.* If the library does not have space for a program, a local business may have a board room rarely used after hours, or a club may have a meeting hall. The Peoria (IL) Public Library reports that successful programs which began in the library move on to other facilities when the library begins a new project. A case in point is a mystery

discussion group which now meets around town at various locations suitable to the book being discussed (e.g. police squad room).

- *Publicity.* Each of the collaborating groups does a share of the promotional work. Because each is publicizing to their own primary constituencies, people who may not be library users (or recipients of your usual publicity materials) will hear about the program.
- *Scheduling.* As Helen Cox of Human Pursuits puts it "By definition, scheduling means working with other organizations."
- *Audience.* Borrowing audiences—to supplement the library's own patrons—is an easy way to ensure attendance at your program. As we'll discuss in Chapter IV, anxiety about attendance is many programmers' number one concern.

Of course the library has much to offer other agencies in return. Often we take ourselves for granted, but studies show that others don't. The library is a highly respected community institution with a great deal to contribute. Besides the collection, the building, and human resources, the library is valued for its neutrality, credibility, and visibility. Keep in mind that the library disseminates local information (e.g. community bulletin board and brochure racks), is supported by a strong constituency, and has specialized expertise that few other agencies can claim. It is essential that cooperation work in both directions. For example, the library cannot expect active participation of the school district if the library is not willing to serve on their committees as well.

There are two other major ways in which collaboration pays off:

- *Enthusiastic support.* When plans are not going as smoothly as hoped, the other organization(s) offer encouragement. Or, at the least, they offer a strong reason not to give up!
- *Political realities.* When the program needs support from local, regional, or national government, the inclusion of various agencies is significant. For example, if a funding request must pass the city council, your partner at parks and recreation might be the agency which can win approval. Or if your state humanities council is considering a grant, having the museum as a partner may help them see your proposal's value.

In other words, community collaboration has valuable philosophical as well as practical bases. I cannot recommend it strongly enough.

Where might you look for community collaborators? Look for partners in the humanities field your program will focus on. The best match is a group whose interests, constituents, and/or goals match yours. For example, if you are doing literary programs, contact local book discussion groups, book stores, poetry organizations, community college English departments, literacy programs. If your program is art-related try the art museum, high school art teachers, and the art society. For public policy programs, contact the League of Women Voters, political action organizations, and civic clubs. For performance programs, talk to the theater, theatrical groups at schools, TV stations and so on.

For any humanities programs, consider:

- American Association of University Women
- Universities, colleges, community colleges and high schools
- Civic clubs such as the Kiwanis, Knights of Columbus, Rotary
- Media including the newspapers, radio and television stations
- Historical societies, museums, and cultural groups
- Bookstores, music and art stores, coffeehouses, restaurants
- Parent/Teacher Associations
- Retired Teachers Associations and other retirement organizations
- Senior centers and housing complexes

And of course you will want to include the Friends of the Library, trustees, literacy programs, and other libraries.

## DECIDING WHETHER TO DEVELOP YOUR OWN PROGRAM

Prepackaged or homegrown?

The decision whether to use a pre-designed program or to develop your own must be made early on. "Homegrown" programs—designed by a representative planning committee—have the advantage of built-in local interest and commitment. If they are based on a special local collection, your access to that resource is another advantage. But pre-designed programs offer many benefits, especially to novice programmers.

So-called "packaged programs" have already selected themes, materials and discussion questions. They usually include professionally produced promotional materials and pragmatic manuals. Often the materials themselves—exhibits, videos, books—are available for loan or rent. Locally, the library must find presenters, scholars and/or discussion leaders, schedule the programs, plan publicity and book distribution strategies, and administer the actual series.

Overall, planning is much easier when using an imported program. As one librarian says: "It is far simpler to use materials which have been developed by another agency such as ALA or NEH: they give you a built-in framework, and sympathetic help is generally available." Another cautions: "Don't reinvent the wheel. There are great program packages you can borrow."

Sixty-seven of the survey respondents create some programs in-house, but most of these originally used programs created elsewhere and currently use ready-made programs as well as their own. Librarians report that using imported programs is good preparation for designing their own. As one librarian reports: "In each instance, the model has been similar: another organization has provided the general framework, and we have plugged in our own local resources, talent, and concept. We have found this a very successful way to work."

## THEME DEVELOPMENT

Many librarians have experience in adult (or youth) recreational programming which requires only passive involvement from the audience such as watching a performance. In humanities programs, although the initial activity may be entertaining (e.g. a play, reading, or film), the purpose is not recreation but contemplation and growth. The participants are expected to be actively engaged in consideration of and discussion on human concerns. Therefore, the most significant question in planning humanities programs are these: How do we engage the participants? What theme or topic will generate the necessary interest?

Note that one-third of the survey respondents use pre-designed programs borrowed from the American Library Association, National Council on the Aging, Centers for the Book and other groups. If you and your planning committee decide to use a program which has already been developed—for example, one of those highlighted in Chapter 7—you can skip this part of the planning process. Move directly to *Planning a Pre-designed Series* on page 51.

If you decide to develop your own theme, you'll probably find that this is the most enjoyable step in planning. Most of the survey respondents marked "selecting the topic" as their favorite task; seventy-seven percent reported that discussing and deciding on themes was the most fun the planning process offers. As Pat Bates, the originator of "Let's Talk About It" reports: "The most fun for me is sitting with a group of scholars and librarians and dreaming up ideas (themes) and discussing what books fit into the themes. I could spend my life planning programs—it's doing them that's difficult!"

Selecting a theme or topic for your series takes much time and consideration, but it is important not to skimp in this part of the planning as the rest is dependent on this choice.

## HUMANITIES PERSPECTIVES

Some issues have inherent values that fall naturally into the perspective of humanities. For example, questions of censorship and intellectual freedom simply cannot be discussed without reference to values, whether those of a particular group such as the Moral Majority or those innate to the First Amendment. Questions abound: What are community standards? Traditional values? The role of the library—and of parents—in perpetuating society's values? It would be almost impossible to limit a program on intellectual freedom to a discussion of court decisions. By the very nature of the topic, the humanities—literature, religion, philosophy—must come into play.

On the other hand, it is possible to present a program on technical issues that is limited to technological information. Yet even a technology program can be given a humanities emphasis because society cannot make decisions on technology without considering human factors. For example, a humanities-based discussion of nuclear energy must consider human questions (e.g. is it preferable to risk war with oil producing countries to avoid the possibility of nuclear contamination?) as well as scientific facts (e.g. what is the technical likelihood of a reactor leak?).

A first-time program planner may want to select a "natural" humanities theme such as "the changing role of women as viewed in literature." Such a program might consist of discussion of novels from the nineteenth and twentieth centuries which show women's roles changing over time. Jane Austen, Henrik Ibsen, Tolstoy, Doris Lessing and others might be included. After developing such a topic, the planner can move on to more difficult themes. Keep in mind, though, that since the humanities are inherent to all human concerns, you should not be daunted by topics which are not immediately apparent as humanities related. A humanistic perspective can be brought to the discussion of any topic. Ask yourself these questions about the topic at hand:

- What can we learn from the past about this?
- What have authors, poets, playwrights said about this issue in their writings?
- What religious beliefs might be affected by the issue?
- Have philosophers through the ages speculated about it?
- What are the social implications for women? Men? Children? Elders? Families? The community as a whole?

## THE COLLECTION AS INSPIRATION

Let your collection be your inspiration.

One approach to developing a theme is to focus on your library's unique resources or special collections. Such materials can provide inspiration to you, and the programs which result will introduce those resources to a larger audience which will value them in a new way. In other words, the programs can exploit your resources to the fullest while encouraging wider access and use.

Often exhibits are developed out of special collections. By themselves, exhibits can be informative and enjoyable, but their value as humanities programs is greatly increased when discussion is added. Discussion programs are a natural outgrowth of exhibits because they typically raise questions that demand human interaction to conceive of answers. For example, the Newberry Library—a private research library in Chicago—received an NEH grant in 1988 to develop an exhibit about the Arthurian legend with manuscripts and artifacts from its own collection of Arthuriana. One goal was to encourage consideration of how the legend has been reinterpreted over time and retold in a variety of literary guises. Another purpose was to allow the public to view this special collection. The exhibit has been traveling throughout the US since 1995 and has a *Let's Talk About It* reading and discussion series to complement it.

Your "special resources" need not be as esoteric as those in the Newberry Library. What about your mystery novel collection? Indeed, many public libraries have designed discussion series based on popular detective novels. The Southern Connecticut Reading Council, in their successful proposal to NEH, stressed that mysteries are written and read because of a need for meaning: Edgar Allan Poe was said to have invented the detective story to allay his suspicions that the world was meaningless. "Detectives are seekers after truth, and the satisfaction that readers derive from detective fiction parallels the kind of satisfaction that scientists, researchers, and thinkers of all kinds seek in their work . . . What the fiction does is to reaffirm the value of the search for truth and to provide the vicarious pleasure of a successfully completed search." The proposal also presented the idea that detective novels fill a need for humans to distinguish right from wrong, and "to admit to the existence of guilt and the power of the human mind to cope with it" (Phelps).

"Popular fiction, popular art in general, is the very air a civilization breathes." Ross Macdonald

The Council quotes the author Ross Macdonald "Popular fiction, popular art in general, is the very air a civilization breathes . . . Popular art is the form in which a culture comes to be known by most of its members. It is the carrier of the spoken language. A book which can be read by everyone, a convention which is widely used and understood in all its variations, holds a civilization together as nothing else can." Can you see the natural humanities content—ethics, philosophy, classics—of a program on mysteries? Some of the discussion questions for the detective novel series were: Discuss the detective as knight errant, the moral force in a corrupt world. Discuss the role of the detective as an observer rather than a participant in life. How does the social class of the detective affect the actions he can take to solve a crime? How have the rules of detective fiction changed over the years and how do these changes affect reader identification with the detective? Compare the satisfaction the reader derives from solving the crime to that deriving from involvement in the character's life. Have tough moral choices replaced traditional detection? Does that bring the reader closer to the protagonist? Do we accept a higher level of violence from the good guy? Discuss the ways in which the detective participates in, operates outside of, or functions in opposition to the official system of justice (Phelps).

## COMMUNITY INTERESTS

Another approach to creating a theme is to look at the issues facing your community. For example, has the latest census underlined a changing demographic? What are the ramifications of these changes? Or, is an upcoming election stressing issues which merit discussion beyond the directly political?

Do not underestimate the interests hidden in your community.

Do not underestimate the interests hidden in your community. As the small town of Venice, Florida reports "You'd be surprised at people's interests. Fifty people showed up for our first poetry discussion—in a town of 15,000." As the library in Medina, Ohio considered the *Poets in Person series*, "we wondered if Medina residents would be interested. A bit skeptically, we made inquiries of community cultural and service groups . . . Again and again we were met with enthusiastic support . . . Because of our small meeting room, registration was limited to 30 but our average attendance was 34."

A Maryland programmer writes "I could develop endless projects on American history and they'd all be popular. I'm amazed at the hunger for learning about our country's history." Connecticut's experience is similar, and reports that men especially are interested in history. Although women comprise 80% of most of their book discussion group audiences, the audience for history-based topics was 42% men.

## PROCESS

The first step in theme development is brainstorming by the planning committee. (You may decide to invite a few extra humanists to the session to have a diversity of ideas.) Sally Anderson, the director of the Vermont Center for the Book, advises against asking the committee "What do you want to do?" Instead, she recommends, give your members parameters such as "The program should focus on books and require the library's involvement." Or "It should tie in to the local festivities and foster discussion."

Once you've developed a list of potential topics, narrow your list by asking all of these questions:

- Will the theme have relevance to your community (e.g. geographic, or ethnic)?
- Will it appeal particularly to your target audience (e.g. older adults, or an intergenerational mix)?
- Will the theme appeal to both men and women? (If not, is that acceptable given your goals?)
- Will it provoke constructive controversy and discussion?
- Will the theme allow for a diversity of opinions and a range of books and authors?
- Will it encourage participants to use other materials and services which the library offers?

Now narrow further by combining topics which have a common thread into one larger theme. For example, when planning the original *Let's Talk About It* themes, the committee generated these topics: identity, unemployment, employment, professions, leisure time, and retirement. Since they were all associated with the concept of working, working became a program series theme. Note that the theme may not be the title. In the case above, "Making A Living, Making A Life" was the title of the series on the working theme.

## PROGRAM FORMATS

Humanities programs can take many forms. Popular program formats include:

- Exhibits
- Lectures
- Chautauquas and other living history events
- Dramatic readings or performances
- Symposia
- Video or audio presentations
- Public discussions

Discussion programs, which by definition value the individual's contribution, are quintessential humanities programs. They are especially relevant to the library's mission to serve readers. Readers believe that books are both windows out (as Tuchman said) and into the self. Discussion programs, which value the reader's personal responses to reading as well as the literal content of the books read, provide readers with a much sought after outlet for their reactions to books, for the combination of open dialogue and private introspection.

Discussion groups differ from other programming in three significant ways. First, whether based on reading, viewing, or listening—or a combination of those—discussion groups encourage both the contemplation of ideas and the sharing of them with others. Second, discussion groups value both the humanist (or scholar's) point of view and that of the individual participants, while other humanities formats concentrate only on the scholar's expertise. Last, other programs allow the audience to be passively engaged while discussion requires each person to be actively involved.

I've been told that "active discussion" is an oxymoron, but I heartily disagree. Richard A. Lewis, in his *Discussing the Humanities* argues "Humanities discussion programs represent an activity that is essential to our survival as a free people . . . We sometimes hear discussion dismissed as idle, nonactive, a waste of time in a busy world. We are told that what is needed to solve our problems is action. But, when it is well conducted, discussion *is* action. Discussion is growth, clarification, self-discovery, change, understanding, and any combination of these and other 'events'" (Lewis, pp. 4–5).

Lewis' argument echoes that of Hannah Arendt in *Men in Dark Times*: "We humanize what is going on in the world and in our-

---

"Active discussion" is not an oxymoron . . .

"Humanities programs represent an activity that is essential to our survival as a free people." Richard A. Lewis

"We humanize what is going on in the world and in ourselves only by speaking of it, and in the course of speaking of it, we learn to be human." Hannah Arendt

selves only by speaking of it, and in the course of speaking of it, we learn to be human" (Arendt, p. 25).

There is still one more compelling reason for libraries to provide discussion-oriented programs: they are rewarding. As Frannie Ashburn, director of the North Carolina Center for the Book, says, public discussion programs enable librarians to do what they do best: connect people with books. People are hungry for the experience of talking about what they read, and this programming enables them to talk with friends or acquaintances and also with people they'd never meet or never talk to otherwise. And everyone is talking about IDEAS, not something we have the opportunity to do every day. We learn about books from what others have to say, and we learn about others when they talk about the books, and we learn about ourselves every step of the way . . . Good reading, good conversation, the opportunity to learn about life, and it's fun (have I mentioned that?)"

Most humanities discussion programs offered by libraries are based on reading: fiction or non-fiction, anthologies or full texts. An increasingly popular approach is discussion based on viewing: live theater, films & videos, television, exhibits. Others are based on listening: lectures, radio broadcasts, readings. All of these formats have advantages and limitations which must be taken into account.

## BOOKS AND OTHER READINGS

*Advantages:*
- Familiarity by the public.
- Library collections by definition include them.
- Each participant can read at his/her own pace.
- Portability.
- Inexpensive.
- Reading is done prior to the session so program time can be shorter.

*Limitations:*
- Reading material must be acquired in quantity so that each participant has a copy to use. Otherwise, a sharing system among participants must be designed.
- All participants must be literate. Otherwise, alternative formats (e.g. audiocassette versions) must be available.
- The physical format (e.g. standard type, hardcover) must be acceptable to all participants. Otherwise, alternative formats (e.g. large type, Braille) must be available.

## FILM, VIDEO, AND TV

*Advantages:*
- Familiarity by the public.
- Accessible to literate and non-reading people.
- Viewing can be done prior to the session so program time can be shorter.
- May add emotional impact to material.

*Limitations:*
- If viewing is not done prior to the session, program time must be lengthened to allow sufficient time for viewing and discussion.
- Equipment (projector, VCR, or TV) must be available in-house and for loan.
- Multiple copies must be acquired for loan.
- Scheduled showings must be offered for participants who do not have their own equipment.

## LECTURES:

*Advantages:*
- Participants can attend without preparation (e.g. reading or viewing) beforehand.
- Well-known speaker can draw an audience.
- Knowledge of reading and ability to read print are not required.

*Limitations:*
- May need larger room than for discussion-only
- Need amplification system.
- Success dependent on skill of speaker.
- Program time must be longer to allow time for lecture and discussion.

## DRAMATIC READING OR PERFORMANCE

*Advantages:*
- Participants can attend without preparation (e.g. reading or viewing) beforehand.
- Knowledge of reading and ability to read print are not required.
- May attract a different audience.
- Live performances add emotional impact.

*Limitations:*
- Need larger room than for discussion-only
- Need amplification system.
- May need stage and props.
- Success dependent on skill of readers/actors.
- Program time must be longer to allow time for performance and discussion.
- Cost may be high.

## EXHIBITS

*Advantages:*
- Viewing can be done prior to the session so program time can be shorter.
- May attract a different audience.

*Limitations:*
- Need space for exhibit.
- Cost of shipping (or original production), installation, and insurance.
- If viewing is not done prior to the session, program time must be lengthened to allow sufficient time for viewing and discussion.
- May require interpretation to some participants.
- Success dependent on quality of exhibit.

# BOOK SELECTION FOR DISCUSSION PROGRAMS

Once you have a theme, it is time to select the books—and other materials—which will be the basis of the program. Librarians (and scholars) usually delight in this activity for it draws upon all their professional skills. As one librarian states: "This is exciting and interesting, as we always read the best titles . . . I always enjoy this activity." Another writes: "I enjoy the creative process of engaging ideas on texts with prospective participants."

Before creating a "laundry list" of wonderful books related to your theme, decide on the number of titles you want to use in your series. The *Let's Talk About It* themes typically had five books, but Sally Anderson of the Vermont Center for the Book reports that their series now have four books and that audiences appreciate the shorter reading list and fewer discussions per series.

Here are some questions to consider as you select books:

- Will the book stimulate serious discussion? This is the most important question of all. The book should generate enough debate to sustain a two hour program and should raise questions that give rise to legitimate differences of opinion.
- What is the book's appeal? Is it informational, humorous, inspirational? Does it stimulate an intellectual response or a more personal one? Note that imaginative literature (e.g. fiction, drama, poetry) usually strikes a different note than didactic literature (e.g. essays, biography, other non-fiction). Both are equally interesting, but may appeal to different people so a mixture of types is recommended. Consider using numerous genres so that everyone's favorite is included. Experienced programmers advise "Don't underestimate your patrons."
- How difficult is the book? If it is too difficult, some people may give up, not finish it and so will not be able to participate fully. If it is too easy, some participants may not feel challenged, not finish it, and not be able to participate. Again, a mixture of levels of difficulty is probably best unless you are certain of the reading levels of your target group.
- Can the book be read comfortably within the time allotted? Is there a balance in your series between short and lengthy books?
- Who is the author? Do your authors reflect the diversity in your target audience? In your community? One common criticism of humanities programs is their emphasis on "dead white males."
- Is the book in print? The shelf life of books has greatly decreased over the past few years as tax laws have caused publishers to shorten their backlists. If the book is not in print, do not use it unless the library is positive that it can provide enough copies. Nothing is as frustrating to participants as being unable to find the required book. Most programmers recommend eliminating all books which are not in print and readily available.
- Is the book available in paperback? It is not essential that the books be in paperback and sometimes it is important to include books which are too new to have been released

in paperback. But paperbacks are much less expensive and easier to handle than hardcover books, important considerations if your library must buy multiple copies or if you are asking individual participants to purchase their own copies.

- Is the book available in large type and/or on cassette? As our society ages, more people are needing large type or audio versions. Note that cassettes are also popular with joggers and commuters.
- Does the book tie in with other activities your library or other community agencies offer?
- Does your library own enough copies to respond to the demands of nonparticipants who may also want to read the publicized titles?
- Does your library own—or can it gain access to—other materials that respond to the interest this book may arouse (e.g. in other works by the same author or from the same era)?

Based on your answers to the above questions, develop selection criteria for your committee to use in selecting books. Again, begin by brainstorming and then narrow the list. Next assign the titles to members of the committee for reading and evaluation before a final selection meeting.

# BOOK DISTRIBUTION

One of your primary concerns will be to ensure that participants have copies of the titles chosen for the series. You can do this in one of three main ways:

- *The program provides the books.* Ideally you would provide one book for each participant for each program. If this is impossible, books may be shared by participants by creating a buddy system among members, by allowing only truncated loans, or by arranging for some participants to read some books while some read others. Keep in mind that besides the library's own copies, you may be able to borrow individual copies from other libraries through interlibrary loan or groups of books from a special rotating collection. For example, Kate Oser of the Southern Connecticut Library Council reports that they have 30 copies of each title for 55 themes; the books are loaned to libraries when they do a program. You may be able to purchase a collection of titles inexpensively at used book stores, or at any bookstore with funds from a local merchant or through a grant. You may also be able to have books donated by a local bookstore.

Note that many pre-planned programs include multiple copies of the reading materials—to borrow or to rent—in the agreement. For example, the "Discovery Through the Humanities" project of the National Council on the Aging, Inc. rents 8–25 copies of their books to a library for a $50 fee. The National Issues Forum sells copies of their materials. And a number of states and local programs will loan copies of their reading and discussion titles to other libraries.

- *Participants purchase their own copies.* If you take this approach, be sure to alert the local bookstores as far in advance as possible so that they can meet the demand. Request that program participants receive a discount price, or that the store donate a few copies for participants who are unable to afford them. Many bookstores will work with you in exchange for the business and publicity you bring them. If you do not have a bookstore in town, or do not have a cooperative one, you may choose to order multiple copies from a jobber and then sell them to the participants, passing along the savings or using the "profit" to purchase copies for loan. In any case, be sure to provide free or reserve copies for participants who cannot afford to purchase them.
- *Create your own materials.* Some libraries, groups of libraries, and other agencies have created their own readings. For example, the Rhode Island Committee for the Humanities created an anthology of short stories for use by libraries and others. In addition, they hired an actress to read two of the stories onto cassette, copies of which were loaned to participants. The Minnesota Center for the Book has received permission to copy passages of books and has distributed those.

# AV MATERIALS

Audiovisual materials have proven popular adjuncts to books in national series such as *Voices and Visions* and *Poets in Person*. And in some state and local series, such as Ohio's *Communities at Work*, audiovisual materials have been successfully used on their own.

Films and audiotapes offer many advantages for people who have difficulty reading (e.g. adult new readers, people with learning differences, people with visual impairments) and for people who prefer these genres (e.g. commuters, young adults). In addition, these materials offer more immediate gratification and can be experienced as a group. While their use during a program allows for less reflection than reading a book prior to the session, using audiovisual materials together does guarantee that everyone has seen/heard the material and can discuss it.

Be aware that the use of audiovisual materials may add two additional responsibilities. First, you may need to alter the format of your program. For example, viewing a film may shorten the time available for a presentation or for discussion. One possibility is to reconfigure the group, another is to offer viewing times not during the session, and yet another is to lengthen the session. Second, you will need to make advance arrangements for the materials, equipment, and an operator. You may also need to arrange for different, more suitable locations for viewing/listening.

Many of the criteria for selecting audiovisual materials are the same for those in print because your objective—inclusive, wholehearted discussion—is the same. Be sure to bear in mind the questions listed above. Here are some additional considerations unique to media:

- Is the physical quality of the material adequate?
- Does it cover more than one side of an issue? Films often oversimplify an issue for dramatic reasons, thus compromising their discussion value.
- Are there aspects intrinsic to the material that could distract? E.g. costumes, language, accents, music, quality of the acting?
- Does the material still allow for the viewer's imagination? Or does the presentation of specific actors and settings limit the relevance of the content?

Remember the cardinal rule for using audiovisual materials:

Never use a film, video, or audio recording which you have not previewed.

## SELECTING EXHIBITS

In many cases, selecting the theme *is* selecting the exhibit, because the number of exhibits available on any one topic are few. However, if you have a number of exhibits to choose between, begin by considering these questions:

- Was the exhibit curated by an acknowledged expert in the area?
- Is the physical quality of the objects (or panels) excellent? Clearly this is the most important criteria.
- Are the objects well displayed?
- Are the labels and other interpretive information clear and understandable?
- Does it cover more than one side of an issue?
- Does the library own materials which patrons can use or borrow to further explore the ideas behind the exhibit?
- Does your library have sufficient space for the size of the exhibit?
- Can the library provide adequate (as defined by the lending agency) security?

## SCHEDULING

Far less interesting than theme or materials selection, scheduling is nonetheless equally important. According to survey respondents, it is time-consuming, but not difficult. Use your planning committee to assist you in scheduling—if it has been well selected it will include people who are aware of other activities in the community. As you schedule your programs, take into account the following:

- Regularity. To help your audiences schedule—and remember—your programs, it is best to hold programs on the same day of the week in regularly spaced intervals (e.g. every other Tuesday for eight weeks).

- How frequently will you meet? Most programmers recommend programs every two weeks because weekly programs can seem too demanding and monthly ones may lack continuity. However, this decision must be made based on the needs of the participants (e.g. are they traveling great distances?), the material (e.g. are you allowing enough time for the required reading?), and the library (e.g. availability of space).

- How long will each program last? Two hours is a common length because it allows time for a presentation and ample discussion yet is not long enough to require long breaks or refreshment. The group should be able to explore the materials sufficiently while maintaining a high level of concentration. Experienced programmers say it is better to close a program while interest is still strong rather than letting interest die.

- What time of day? Both the participants' preferences and the library's schedule need to be considered. For example, an audience of retirees may prefer a daytime program while working adults prefer evenings. The library may be open all day, but cramped in the after school hours. One idea that has worked for many libraries is lunch or dinner hour programs where participants bring in their own meal.

- What day of the week? Does your library already offer library programs on an established day? Are certain days reserved for Little League in your town? Is a specific TV program popular in your community? Many library programs are held on Wednesday or Thursday evenings because the middle of the week is often the least scheduled part of people's calendars.

- What competition will you have? Be sensitive to local, state, or national events that might compete with your series. These include elections, sporting events, and symphony or theater schedules. Consider also holidays, weather, and traffic patterns.

- Where will the program be held? Most librarians feel it is preferable to meet *in* the library building so the library is firmly established as a cultural and lifelong learning center. However, some libraries do not have appropriate facilities and must hold programs elsewhere. What public agency or private business has an available, accessible and welcoming meeting room? Also, some libraries are purposely holding programs off-site to attract different audiences. What about a workplace program? Pat Bates claims that 98% of the people who attend her workplace programs never attend programs at the library. Libraries have had great success, too, taking programs into nursing homes and prisons to reach non-library users.

# THE AMERICANS WITH DISABILITIES ACT

In 1990, then-President Bush signed into law new civil rights legislation which directly affects millions of people and indirectly affects us all. The Americans with Disabilities Act (ADA), or PL 101–336, guarantees that people with disabilities shall not be discriminated against on the basis of their disabilities and shall have equal opportunities in employment, public services and accommodations, transportation, and telecommunication services. Most Americans are aware of the law only in its architectural aspects: ramps and accessible bathrooms are sprouting everywhere. But the ADA, which went into effect in 1992, encompasses much more, including public programs.

The services—including special programs—of a public entity such as a library must be accessible by people with disabilities. This means that your planning must include developing methods by which people with hearing or vision loss, as well as mobility disabilities, can participate in your program. You may wish to include in your planning committee a person with a disability, or a representative from an organization or agency serving people with disabilities. Or you may want to consult with your library's ADA Coordinator to be sure that your program is accessible.

A few places to start:

- All print materials, including publicity and readings, should be available in large type. Other formats—such as audiotapes or braille versions—should be made available upon request.
- Any video materials should be open or close captioned for the deaf, and, if possible, described for the blind.
- All meetings, performances, exhibits, etc. should be held in facilities which are wheelchair accessible and have wheelchair accessible bathrooms.
- All publicity should include a statement that accommodations (e.g. sign language interpretation and assistive listening devices) are available for all programs. Typical wording is "Accommodations for people with disabilities will be provided upon request. Please give us two weeks notice."

# SCHOLARS

A scholar in the humanities—also referred to as a "humanist"—is usually defined as one who has a Ph.D. and teaches in a humanities field or whose life is devoted to the study and application of the humanities. Most often, humanities scholars are employed at universities and colleges, but "public service scholarship" is a growing area in which humanists work for the benefit of the broader public, often through humanities councils and other agencies with the goal of bringing scholarly knowledge to the public.

The National Endowment for the Humanities, and the state humanities councils, require the involvement of a scholar in most programs which they fund. The commonly accepted rationale for this requirement is that "the scholar's role is central to humanities programming" to ensure that programs are "informed by scholarship." In other words, programs benefit from involving humanities scholars because they have been trained to use critical thinking and to place ideas in a historical and philosophical context.

The North Dakota Committee for the Humanities and Public Policy states: "Most humanists are gadflies, provokers of discussion, stimulators in reasoning. They do not often see issues in black and white terms; after all, they are professional explorers of the gray area. They compare the past with the present, ask the right questions, separate fact questions from value questions, demonstrate that the 'right' action depends on values, show the importance of some things that have no practical value . . . " (Phelps).

In addition to those reasons, involving a scholar lends the program a certain cachet. As one librarian put it "The scholar is vital . . . Otherwise it's a 'ladies' book group'."

Usually, scholars are included in the planning process and/or are hired to give presentations during the humanities programs. There is disagreement among experienced programmers as to when to involve a scholar—some feel that it is essential to invite them early on, to assist with theme and book selection. Others feel that you cannot select the scholar until you know the content. One solution used by some libraries is to invite one scholar to participate in the planning process and then another scholar to do the presentations.

Most often these presentations are a bridge between the reading (listening, and/or viewing) done by participants and their discussion of the book (or other material). The lecture is to give perspective and context to the material being discussed and to raise questions which will elicit discussion.

"Most humanists are gadflies, provokers of discussion, stimulators in reasoning . . ."
North Dakota Committee for the Humanities and Public Policy

Sometimes scholars are also employed as discussion leaders, but often this is a mistake for three important reasons. First, the scholar is there as a subject specialist, a resource for the discussion participants, and needs to be available to float from group to group. Second, the scholar may not be experienced in discussion leadership, a special process skill, and/or may be too engrossed in content to be an effective process leader. Third, even if s/he is skilled at discussion leadership, the participants may hesitate to share their experiences and opinions in front of an "expert." My recommendation is to separate the roles of scholar and discussion leader, and to value both.

Some programs funded by NEH or state humanities councils have been exempted from the scholar requirement. Due to the remote location of the programs, or a scarcity in scholars in a certain area, permission may be given to hire an academic person with an MA in the field or for another expert, for example a non-degreed author in the field. Other programs have done without scholars—either for the lack of humanists or the lack of funds to pay them—and have found other sources for content expertise in planning the programs. For example, a knowledgeable community member, a secondary school teacher, or a librarian may be pressed into service. And may be equally as capable depending on the subject matter and the person's relation to it. One library reports using "citizens with some expertise in the field being discussed, e.g. a park district naturalist led the discussion of 'Sand County Almanac' and a forensic pathologist led one of the mystery discussions."

The scholar (or other subject specialist) may be accustomed to being the "guest star" in classes and lectures. Yet these programs are more like ensemble work. Here the scholar is an equal partner with the program coordinator, the discussion leaders, and the participants. Of course the scholar is valued for his/her insights into the materials and other humanities sources. But in turn, the scholar must be open to the wealth of experience in the adult audience and must value the work of the coordinator and the discussion leaders. This role may be a new one for the scholar, but if s/he is experienced in working with out-of-school adults, congenial and diplomatic, it will be no problem.

Assuming that you want to include a scholar in the planning and/or the implementation of your programs, a number of questions must be addressed.

- What will the scholar actually do?
- How will you know if a particular scholar is appropriate for your program?

- How can you locate a scholar?
- How do you evaluate a scholar's contribution?

The first two questions should be answered in your preparation of a position description for the scholar. Just as we prepare position descriptions before hiring permanent staff or before locating volunteers, a job description for such a contractual position is vital because it clarifies what you are looking for, what will be required, and how you will know if you have a good fit. A sample follows.

Locating a scholar may seem daunting but doing it carefully will be worthwhile in the long run. Nearly a third of the survey respondents reported that this task is fun; twenty-one percent found it time-consuming but not difficult.

One librarian, however, cautions: "Too often, I think, the assumption with humanities programming is that there are scholars right there in town who have nothing more pressing to do than to present library programs. In many states it is miles and miles between colleges/universities and the faculty are busy with their own lives and classes most of the week . . ." She continues "Just because a person has a Ph.D. doesn't mean that he/she is a good presenter. Of the 30 some scholars we had over the course of 8 years of discussion programs, more than one had barely even read the book, let alone given thought to what would be said. Though when a topic was of particular interest to the scholar s/he would lecture with enthusiasm that would be conveyed to the audience." The lesson from this is: only select scholars who do indeed have a strong interest in your theme or materials.

The first step is to compile a list of potential scholars in your subject area. Contact:

- local colleges and universities (note that numerous respondents assert that community college scholars are usually better at working with the out-of-school adult than university professors.)
- the state humanities council
- the state library
- nearby libraries and other agencies which offer humanities-based programs
- art museums or historical societies depending on the subject area
- any humanist you know from another context

Humanists have informal networks and one may be able to lead you to others more suited to your needs. As Truth Schiffauer, a programmer in the Delmarva (Delaware, Maryland, Virginia) area, reports, "Scholars usually recommend other scholars. At this time, we have about one hundred scholars in the Delmarva area who are willing to or have presented a book discussion." The other regional and state programs (see Chapter 7) also keep lists of scholars with whom they have worked.

One experienced programmer sends a newsletter about her programs to all colleges' English and History departments with a form asking "If you're interested in working with the public on such a program, send your name, address, and resume to . . . "

As you collect names, ask for recommendations. Is the scholar skilled at working with the public? Will s/he stimulate discussion rather than simply lecture? Is s/he dependable? As one librarian put it "The difficult part is not finding scholars but getting accurate assessments about their abilities and experience in working with a wide variety of adults." If at all possible, sit in on a lecture by the candidates. Keep in mind that you will have to work with the scholar, so your personalities as well as your areas of expertise must be complementary. Because of this, arrange telephone appointments to speak with each of the potential scholars and use that opportunity to ask about his/her experience in working with out-of-school adults. Then have face-to-face interviews to discuss your initial ideas; if you feel that s/he does not seem excited by the issues, may not relate well to your community, or may not work well with you, arrange for an interview with the next person on the list. And so on. It is as if you are hiring temporary but essential staff for your library—and the hiring process is important.

When your program is over, be sure to assess the work of the scholar. One way to evaluate the scholar's contribution is to ask the participants about his/her participation (see Chapter 5). Then ask yourself these questions. Did the scholar:

- talk *with* or *at* the public?
- create interest in the topic?
- serve as a resource person or a dominant lecturer?
- stimulate discussion among participants?
- respect the contributions of the public?
- bring to the discussion something beyond the material read (or experienced)?
- enjoy him/herself?

## SCHOLAR: JOB DESCRIPTION

To be an equal partner in the presentation of a humanities-based discussion program at the public library for out-of-school-adults.

To be a humanities resource, to offer insights into the materials, to broaden the humanities experience for the participants.

To elicit audience involvement, to value the life experiences of the participants, to provide a mutually rewarding interchange.

## MINIMUM QUALIFICATIONS

- An advanced degree in the humanities. In some cases an MA will suffice; in others, a Ph.D. will be necessary.
- Professionally engaged in—or retired from—teaching, writing, researching, or studying in the humanities.
- Clear evidence of continuing scholarly endeavor.
- Background appropriate to the subject matter of the program.
- Enthusiasm about humanities programs.
- Experience in public programs, not just classroom situations.
- Time to fulfill the demands of the program.
- Personality requirements: friendly, diplomatic, tactful, good communication skills.

## PREFERRED EXTRA QUALIFICATIONS

- Previous participation in library programs.
- Previous experience as a scholar in other humanities programs in libraries.

## RESPONSIBILITIES

- Assist planning committee in theme development and selection of formats and materials.
- Prepare and deliver a 30 –40 minute presentation, plus discussion questions, on the material to be discussed.
- Meet with coordinator and discussion leaders two weeks before the program about the discussion questions and the program agenda.
- Prepare autobiographical information—about two paragraphs—for coordinator to use in introducing you.
- Circulate among participants during the discussion period.
- Wrap up the discussion at the end of the program.
- Meet with program coordinator after the program to review impressions.

- Complete evaluation (and any other paperwork such as expense reimbursement requests or time logs) as requested by coordinator.
- Help promote the program series.

## DISCUSSION LEADERS

A discussion leader ensures that each member of the audience can participate and feels valued while keeping the discourse focused on the humanities.

The discussion leader is the third member of the discussion program ensemble. The coordinator is in charge of the planning, and the scholar gives the presentation which sets the tone and the context for the program, but the discussion leader has the crucial responsibility for the discussion by participants. The discussion leader must keep the audience interested and involved. S/he ensures that each member of the audience can participate and feels valued while keeping the discourse focused on the humanities. The importance of this role cannot be overemphasized—a good discussion leader can salvage even poorly selected material while a weak discussion leader can abuse even the best material.

Many discussion programs do not use separate leaders; these programs rely on the scholar to serve as discussion leader. If the audience is not large enough to break into small groups, or if a medium-sized audience (30 people) is broken into two groups, one of whom is led by the coordinator, discussion leaders may not be needed. Another situation when leaders are not necessary is the short workplace program, typically 45 minutes total. Also, one librarian suggests that "information-dense books work best with the scholar as discussion leader."

Some survey respondents advise keeping the audience small enough to avoid breaking into discussion groups. As one librarian says "I hate breaking up and having to move everybody." Another agrees: "Sometimes we want to divide into small groups following the scholar's lecture, but it can be a real headache, finding the discussion leaders and training them . . . " A third reports: "People don't want to commit to having to come to every session and to have to lead—they want to participate, not just facilitate. There's usually not enough time for the discussion leader to meet with discussion leaders prior to the program, especially when the scholar comes from 30–some miles away . . . Most of the scholars had not grasped the discussion leader concept, either . . . "

For the majority of programs, though, I highly recommend separate discussion leaders. People are much more willing to share their ideas in a small group, scholars are able to circulate among the groups to get the "feel of the discussion," and discussion leaders are usually better able to deflect attention from their views onto that of the participants.

One way to avoid the discussion leader/ no discussion leader quandary is to co-lead the discussion yourself. Libraries report that a medium-sized audience can effectively exchange and debate ideas with the scholar and coordinator co-leading.

The discussion leader need not be an authority on the subject, but must be a process expert. Central to this are her or his listening skills, diplomacy, responsibility, and ability to think and act quickly to keep the discussion on track and the participants involved. Many people in your community have these qualities. To find them, ask:

- planning committee members
- library staff
- library board members
- school board members
- civic clubs which hold discussions (e.g. AAUW, League of Women Voters)
- local book clubs
- volunteer bureau
- community agencies
- historical societies and museums

A number of libraries report that they recruit discussion leaders from the participants of previous programs. Frannie Ashburn, director of the Center for the Book in North Carolina, says that she recruits discussion leaders by inviting participants to an onsite information session for potential discussion leaders about two weeks before the programs. Other libraries recruit volunteers from the program registrants and so are able to train them ahead of time. Still others ask people in the audience to lead a group; I personally do not recommend trusting fate to provide the right number of willing and able volunteers right when you need them.

Some libraries have also located discussion leaders through churches and schools, but clergy and teachers often have too didactic a bent to be exemplary discussion leaders. People whose experience and training have taught them to lecture, persuade, or control an audience may not be the best candidates. On the other hand, certain professions may have equipped their members with just the skills you are seeking.

Once you have compiled a list of candidates, check their references as you did for the scholar. Try to see (or have a trusted colleague see) the candidates leading a group discussion in another context. Remember, you are looking for someone who can listen to other people's opinions without trying to impose his or her own, someone who is tactful, who provides all participants with the opportunity to speak, and who maintains a sense of poise and responsibility.

The number of discussion leaders you will need for any one program depends on the size of your audience. Eight to ten participants is a good size for small-group discussion; fifteen is an outside limit.

Here are some questions to ask yourself as you decide on discussion leaders:

- Will this person enjoy the program?
- Will s/he be enthusiastic?
- Will s/he avoid imposing their own opinions on the group?
- Will s/he be able to handle strong differences of opinions within the group?
- Will s/he lead the group to consider the topic in different ways?
- Will s/he ask thought-provoking questions (beyond those provided by the scholar)?
- Will s/he be responsible?

Once you have selected discussion leaders, train them. Unless they are experienced in leading humanities discussion, you need to do at least a short training on their responsibilities, tips on how to deal with difficult group members, and how to use the scholar's questions as well as generate their own.

## DISCUSSION LEADER: JOB DESCRIPTION

### MINIMUM QUALIFICATIONS
- Interest in group discussion.
- Experience as a discussion group participant.
- Respect for opinions of others.
- Ability to be objective.
- Ability to inspire other to think and express themselves.
- Imagination.
- Interest in the humanities content.
- Listening skills, perceptiveness, tact.

### PREFERRED EXTRA QUALIFICATIONS
- Experience as a discussion leader.
- Experience in the humanities.

### RESPONSIBILITIES
- Keep participants alert and interested.
- Encourage participation by all.
- Allow everyone an opportunity to speak.
- Value all contributions to the exchange.
- Ask stimulating questions.
- Maintain the group's focus on the topic at hand, and on the humanities perspective.

# TRAINING/ORIENTATION

No matter how experienced your scholars and discussion leaders are, providing training in public discussion programs is essential. The training workshop is an opportunity to acquaint them with the purposes of the program as well as with the procedures. It provides for review of the essential communication and group process skills. It allows people to learn from each other's prior experiences. It gives advisory committee members, scholars, and discussion leaders a chance to meet each other and to ask questions of each other before the series begins. And, most importantly, it gives everyone a taste of what the program will actually be.

One experienced programmer advises "We have substituted the term 'demonstration program/orientation' for the word 'training' to soothe the Ph.D. egos." She goes on to relate that "demonstrations are invaluable . . . reading and discussion is something you *do* and at a workshop you give the scholars and discussion leaders a chance to *do* what they are going to provide later for others . . . I tell them it's their chance to move around to the other side of the desk/lectern for a while! It's also a chance to model 'ain't we got fun behavior.'"

Numerous librarians report that they require attendance at an orientation before paying any honoraria. A backup plan is to require each scholar and discussion leader to attend a similar program at another library.

# PLANNING CALENDAR

This calendar is offered only as a guide. Depending on your choices of program and format type, your programming experience, and your local resources, you must devise your own calendar. This one—and the checklists which follow—will assist you in planning a realistic schedule.

*Eight Months in Advance*
- Verify administrative support
- Decide on program coordinator
- Plan collaboration approach
- Contact potential partners and co-sponsors
- Identify planning committee members
- Prepare preliminary project budget

*Seven Months in Advance*
- Planning meeting(s) to determine goals, select theme and format(s), finalize budget
- Identify funding sources
- Verify in-kind contributions necessary from library and other sponsors
- Write position descriptions as necessary

*Six Months in Advance*
- Planning meetings to select materials, plan schedule, etc.
- Hire staff if necessary
- Identify site for program; make contact
- Contact potential scholars, discussion leaders, etc.
- Publicity plan; establish publicity committee if necessary

*Five Months in Advance*
- Firm up all decisions
- Contract with scholars, discussion leaders, etc.
- Begin preparation of any materials (e.g. readers)

*Three Months in Advance*
- Begin publicity
- Develop work sheets, time sheets, contributions logs, etc.
- Design evaluation forms

*Two Months in Advance*
- Library staff meeting
- Letters of invitation to potential participants

*One Month In Advance*

- Training for scholars, discussion leaders, etc.

- Intensive publicity including any special events
- Begin registration for participants
- Arrange for refreshments

*Two Weeks in Advance*
- Arrange for ASL interpreters, assistive listening devices, etc. if necessary
- Write introductions for speakers, etc.
- Continue publicity efforts

*One Week in Advance*
- Arrange for reporters at first program

# PLANNING A HOMEGROWN PROGRAM SERIES: A CHECKLIST

\_\_\_ Select planning committee; invite them to participate
\_\_\_ Review goals set by program director
\_\_\_ Brainstorm themes
\_\_\_ Select theme
\_\_\_ Find partner agencies and/or business sponsors
\_\_\_ Develop criteria for materials selection
\_\_\_ Nominate titles
\_\_\_ Assign reading of suggested titles to committee members
\_\_\_ Choose list of books
\_\_\_ Create a name for the series
\_\_\_ Choose dates and times for series
\_\_\_ Write job descriptions and contracts for scholars
\_\_\_ Suggest possible scholars and discussion leaders
\_\_\_ Interview them
\_\_\_ Choose scholars and discussion leaders
\_\_\_ Plan publicity strategy
\_\_\_ Plan budget and develop worksheets, time sheets, and contributions log (see Chapter 3)
\_\_\_ Decide on book distribution policy
\_\_\_ Develop a checklist of implementation tasks, with dates and person responsible. Include:

    Order books as necessary
    Reserve meeting rooms
    Write introduction to series
    Develop bibliography of supplementary materials
    Create visual displays
    Implement publicity plan
    Fundraising
    Order necessary equipment (e.g. AV)
    Arrange for refreshments
    Train discussion leaders
    Train scholars
    Liaison with scholars

\_\_\_ Manage the program
\_\_\_ Evaluate the program
\_\_\_ Keep notes on everything you did (or should have done differently) to help you next time.

# PLANNING A PRE-DESIGNED PROGRAM SERIES: A CHECKLIST

___ Select planning committee; invite them to participate

___ Review goals set by program director

___ Select series

___ Find partner agencies and/or business sponsors

___ Create a name for the series, if necessary

___ Choose dates and times for series

___ Write job descriptions and contracts for scholars and discussion leaders

___ Suggest possible scholars and discussion leaders

___ Interview them

___ Choose scholars and discussion leaders

___ Plan publicity strategy

___ Plan budget and develop worksheets, time sheets, and contributions log (see Chapter 3)

___ Decide on book distribution policy

___ Develop a checklist of implementation tasks, with dates and person responsible. Include:
  Order books as necessary
  Reserve meeting rooms
  Write introduction to series
  Develop bibliography of supplementary materials
  Create visual displays
  Implement publicity plan
  Fundraising
  Order necessary equipment (e.g. AV)
  Arrange for refreshments
  Train discussion leaders
  Train scholars
  Liaison with scholars

___ Manage the program

___ Evaluate the program

___ Keep notes on everything you did (or should have done differently) to help you next time.

# 3 FUNDING AND BUDGETING

## FUNDING

### NATIONAL ENDOWMENT FOR THE HUMANITIES AND STATE HUMANITIES COUNCILS

In the past, most libraries doing humanities programs received all or most of their funding from the National Endowment for the Humanities (NEH) or their state council on the humanities. The NEH or state council funding (or a combination of the two) came to the library either directly (through receipt of a grant) or indirectly (through inclusion in a state, regional, or national program which was funded by a grant from NEH and/or state council funding). All the libraries were required to find in-kind contributions to the project (e.g. staff time, photocopying) and many also raised some cash, often through the Friends of the Library or the library's foundation. But the majority of funding for most library-based humanities programming came from NEH.

The NEH was founded in 1965 and has had four divisions—education, preservation and access, public programs, and research programs—all of which awarded grants. The mission of the Division of Public Programs has been "to enrich individual lives, enhance the common good, and promote effective citizenship by enabling people to assess values and ideas" (National Endowment for the Humanities, Division of Public Programs, 1994, p. 5). The goals have been "to give access to public humanities programs to all Americans, to offer excellence in programming, to exhibit national leadership in the realm of public humanities, and to encourage the educational role of cultural institutions and organizations" (National Endowment for the Humanities, Division of Public Programs, 1996, p. 6).

The Division of Public Programs gave grants in four areas: Libraries and Archives, Museums and Historical Organizations, Media, and Special Projects. The libraries and archives section supported "programs designed to stimulate public understanding of the humanities disciplines as tools that anyone may use to interpret and illuminate what it means to be human through activities based on books, documents, manuscripts, or other library or archival materials" (National Endowment for the Humanities,

Division of Public Programs, 1996, p. 6). Project proposals were accepted for two review rounds a year; a thorough evaluation process typically selected approximately one-third of the projects for funding. Approximately 90% of resubmitted applications were also funded so the total of successful proposals was higher than one-third. Grants ranged from $10,000 to $300,000. In 1991, grants to 25 public programs in libraries totaled $2,973,300 (Phelps).

State humanities council grants varied from state to state, but most solicited applications from libraries and others for "mini-grants" or resource grants to support free admission to public humanities programs of short duration. These grants typically ranged from $100 to $2,000, depending on the state's guidelines and the purpose of the grant, and required matching funds or in-kind contributions. Many libraries used these funds for one aspect of a program, for example a speaker's fee and travel expenses, raising the rest of the money elsewhere. State humanities councils also provided competitive grants ranging from $15,000 to $100,000, again depending on the state agency's budget and priorities.

> In the past, most libraries doing humanities programs received all or most of their funding from the National Endowment for the Humanities or their state council on the humanities . . . In 1996, the situation has changed drastically.

In 1996, the situation has changed drastically. The future of NEH and the state councils is uncertain, as the US Congress "reinvents" the role of government in all aspects of American life. The best case scenarios from Washington while this book is being written call for a 38% reduction in the NEH budget. This translates to an even greater cut in the state council budgets (80% of which come from NEH) and less NEH grants to individual institutions such as libraries. NEH has announced that they will continue giving grants, but the program will be different in four significant ways:

- Media, museums, and library grant proposals will be evaluated together. As of 1995, libraries submitted far fewer proposals than did media and museums.
- Fewer grants will be made to individual libraries and to statewide programs; the emphasis will be on regional and national projects.
- Fewer planning grants will be made; the focus will be on implementation.
- More emphasis on cost-sharing and fundraising strategies.

The new guidelines call for proposals with:

- National significance or impact.
- New, expanded, or diversified audiences.
- Collaboration with other groups.
- Use of multiple formats or new technologies.

The following are the criteria for reviewing implementation grant proposals for possible funding by NEH:

- Intellectual content
- Impact and collaboration potential
- Format of program
- Audience (well defined and diverse?)
- Resources (already identified)
- Project staff (well qualified with clearly defined roles?)
- Plan of work (realistic and efficient?)
- Dissemination/distribution plan (realistic?)
- Budget (reasonable and justified?)

(National Endowment for the Humanities, Division of Public Programs, 1996, p. 1).

Because changes at NEH impact ongoing national humanities programs and state humanities councils, predictions are being made for these also. Existing (prepackaged) national humanities programs will probably require more local cash contributions than before, and locally produced humanities programs may have no support at all from current state humanities agencies. In California, the state humanities council is reconsidering its role, and may become more of a "clearinghouse and convener" than a producer and funder.

These changes in government support are particularly disturbing in light of the 1993 survey for the National Cultural Alliance which found that 80% of the American public agreed with the statement "The Arts and Humanities make my local community a better place to live" and 59% agreed that "Being able to enjoy the Arts and Humanities is a necessity rather than a luxury." A solid majority (59%) agreed with the statement that "without public support, the Arts and Humanities would be available only to the wealthy" and 73% said "in spite of economic hardship, public and private support of the Arts and Humanities should not be curtailed."

Although 41% of respondents in the survey reported that someone in their household had contributed money to the Arts and Humanities during the past year, 51% said that "they do not have enough disposable income to participate in the Arts and Humanities," (National Cultural Alliance, pp. 4–8). In light of this, charging the public for humanities programs is not the answer. Charging the public? In the past, such an idea would not have been whispered by librarians – certainly not published in a book—but now many libraries have "fee-for-added- service" and "cost recovery" programs. I, for one, do not believe that libraries should charge admission for humanities programs.

> 73% of the American public agreed with the statement "In spite of economic hardship, public and private support of the arts and humanities should not be curtailed." 1993 survey by the National Cultural Alliance

Grants, corporate sponsorship, and fundraising are the major options.

Community foundations, corporate foundations, and government agencies are three prime possibilities for grants.

So, where else can libraries turn for funding of humanities programs? Grants is one answer. Corporate sponsorship and fundraising activities are two other increasingly popular options.

## FOUNDATION AND GOVERNMENT GRANTS

Community foundations, corporate foundations, and government agencies are three prime possibilities for grants.

Community foundations are non-profit, non-governmental independent grantmaking organizations with funds from a variety of donors. They are administered by a committee or board which is representative of community interests and they concentrate their grantmaking to non-profit organizations in their own city or region. According to funding consultants, community foundations recently have become more pro-active in soliciting proposals in their main areas of interest rather than just responding to requests as they come in. Making, and keeping, a contact at your local community foundation and knowing its priorities for funding are good first steps.

Keep in mind that a major transfer of wealth is occurring in America today: more older adults have more expendable income than in any other era. Because of our tax structure, many of these assets are being transferred to foundations. Meanwhile, the baby boomer generation—the largest group of people the same age to have ever lived—has hit middle age. Many of them are reaching their peak of income and are also contributing money to causes and foundations. The combination of local foundations' mission to assist community organizations and the growing assets controlled by the foundations make them an extremely important resource. To find out about your community foundation, and any other foundations, use the *Foundation Directory* published annually by the non-profit Foundation Center which has libraries in New York, Washington, DC, Cleveland, and San Francisco. They also have deposit collections of all their publications in over 200 "cooperating libraries."

Other publications of special interest are the *National Guide to Funding for Libraries and Information Services* and the *National Guide to Funding in Arts and Culture* both of which are published biennially. You can contact the Foundation Center at (800) 424–9836. Another excellent source for information on grants to non-profit organizations is The Grantsmanship Center located in Los Angeles; it also provides training throughout the country and publishes materials on proposal writing, program planning, and fundraising. The Grantmanship Center can be reached at (800) 421–9512 or (213) 482–9860. *The Big Book of*

*Library Grant Money 1996–1997* published in 1996 by the ALA is also useful.

The Internet has many excellent resources for grant seekers. A good place to start is Internet Resources for Non-Profit Service Organizations (http://www.sils.umich.edu/ nesbeitt/non-profits/ nonprofits.html). Another is the Council of Foundations (http:// www.fdncenter.org/fundproc/). ALA's Fund for America's Libraries maintains a page which includes links to funding sources and additional fundraising information. (http:\\www.ala.org:70/11/ alagophv/alagophvexec/alagophvexecfund).

Another source of grant money is government entities such as the US Institute of Peace which offers financial support for research, education and training, and dissemination of information on international peace and conflict resolution. In their "solicited grants" category, the Institute funds public library reading and discussion programs. The grants are up to $10,000 for a single library or system, and up to $25,000 for a consortium, regional or state library system. Other examples of government grant-making agencies are the US Bicentennial Commission (1976) and the Quincentenary Commission (1992) which gave programs grants in their respective years.

## CORPORATE SPONSORSHIP

Corporate sponsorship of programs is increasingly popular with libraries. Independent local businesses, especially book and record stores, are competing with large national chains which have moved into neighborhoods throughout the country. One claim that chains use to convince local governments to accept them is that chains typically support regional or local community projects through their direct corporate giving programs and their corporate foundations. The direct corporate giving programs are usually controlled regionally; a local store manager makes a recommendation for funding to the regional program director who makes a decision. Some libraries report that this is a fairly simple, fast method of receiving small to mid-sized financial contributions and/or in-kind support. The corporate foundations have more money to spend but typically have a more complex and longer application process. To find out more about both types of corporate giving, contact your local store's manager who can provide information. Because this person may also be the one to advocate for you to a regional or national office, be sure to be knowledgeable and enthusiastic in this initial contact. Follow up your telephone call (or face to face appointment) with a two page letter summarizing your program and request.

To find out more about corporate foundations and corporate giving, use the publications by the Foundation Center, especially their *National Directory of Corporate Giving*, published biennially.

Locally owned businesses also fund local projects. Despite the fact that most independent booksellers and others are losing money to the chains, which have larger advertising budgets and are able to discount merchandise more sharply because of their mass purchasing power, the locally owned businesses are competing in sponsorship of projects related to their community. Book, record, and art stores are clearly allies of humanities programs and therefore also have potential as funding sources.

Pat Martin, former Development Officer at the ALA, recommends also approaching businesses which are not necessarily related to the humanities. She states that businesses are willing to sponsor programs because they need to "borrow" the trust the community has in the public library. She suggests contacting insurance agencies, hospitals, banks, and auto dealers any of which may provide funds for a program in return for their name on your publicity—and the library's in theirs (Martin). For example, the bank's advertisements may say "Proud sponsor of the Anywhere Public Library's Local History Exhibit and Lecture Series." In order to know your local business owners, and for them to know about the library's activities, join the Chamber of Commerce and/or service groups like the Rotary Club.

## FUNDRAISING ACTIVITIES

This book will not try to summarize the many books and articles that have been written on fundraising. The library media is full of stories of large public libraries mounting fundraising dinners, celebrity appearances, galas and such to raise construction and renovation monies. For smaller amounts of cash, simpler fundraisers such as contests, marathon pledges, and readathons are much reported. The basic guideline is that fundraising activities need to bring in 400% of your costs to be worthwhile. In other words, if the activity is not extremely lucrative, forget it. And don't underestimate the amount of staff and volunteer time, as well as corporate sponsorship and local in-kind contributions, you may have to use in order to make any money.

These cautions aside, for guidance in fundraising activities, see *Fundraising for the Small Public Library: A How-To-Do-It Marvel* by James Swan (Neal-Schuman, 1990) or contact the Fund Raising and Financial Development Section (FRFDS) of the Library Administration and Management Association (LAMA) to find out about their "Fundfare" programs and bibliographies.

### FINAL WORDS OF ADVICE

No matter where you turn for funding, the following tips from the Fund for America's Libraries should be useful:

- Develop a project that enhances the mission and goals of your library
- Don't work in a vacuum; establish ownership of the project by involving your library staff and board.
- Learn as much as possible about the potential funder. Does your project meet the goals of the funder?
- Establish your library's credibility and ability to carry out the goals of the project.
- Make your story compelling.
- Think BIG! Define a broad visionary goal.
- Establish measurable objectives and define your plan of work.
- Establish a realistic evaluation plan.
- Tell who else is interested in the project. Do you have other funding?
- Do you have a plan for the future besides the current "ask"?
- Prepare a realistic budget to cover project expenses.
- Include support data that sharpens the picture a potential funder has of your library.

For additional guidance on sources of funding, and assistance in developing applications, contact the Fund for America's Libraries at (800) 545–2433, extensions 5049 or 5050.

# BUDGETING

### DETERMINING COSTS

For new programmers, one of the most difficult aspects of developing programs is knowing how much money will be needed. Although people have tried it, no one has been able to come up with a blanket cost ratio or estimate—i.e. $10 per person per exhibit. There are too many factors: costs are affected by type of program, availability of speakers and volunteers, obtainability of in-kind contributions, need for transportation, and even by geographic location and season.

If you have never planned a program budget before, find someone in your library or community who has. If you do not know whom to ask, contact your humanities council or SCORE. SCORE is the Senior Corps of Retired Executives, a national organization of retired business people who have registered their willingness to assist others with management problems—such as budgeting.

Here are a few worksheets of items you need to cost out. To make them easy to use, there are separate charts for planning and coordination, promotion, program, and evaluation. In each, you must note the current local price for an item or designate it as an in-kind contribution. (In-kind contributions are donations of equipment, supplies, space, staff time, or other items in lieu of financial assistance.) The worksheets are an attempt to remind you of every possible cost; depending on your own program, you may not incur all the costs listed.

When determining the current price for an item, e.g. video rentals, be realistic. Maybe your video supplier has a special offer at the moment so that rentals are lower cost than usual. Do not use that price; it is bound to have returned to the regular price by the time you need to rent a film for your program. Do not "pad" the budget, but do not underestimate costs either. The "operational expenses" area in particular is easy to misjudge; remember that staying in touch with your community partners, sponsors, funders, and scholars is essential and inevitably costs money in the guise of telephone calls or postage. A last hint on calculating all costs: when confronted with numerous estimates, use the average.

# PLANNING AND COORDINATION COSTS

Program coordinator and others salaries (*note positions, % of work time to be devoted to project, annual salary including fringe benefits*):

Bookkeeping and/or fiscal agent fees:

Meeting costs (*includes room rental, mailings, refreshments*):

End of project follow-up expenses (*including thank you letters to staff, volunteers, scholars, funders, partners*):

Operational expenses (*including telephone, postage, office supplies*):

Other:

# PROMOTION COSTS

Program coordinator and others salaries (*note positions, % of work time to be devoted to project, annual salary including fringe benefits*) :


Graphic artist fees:


Printing and duplication costs (*e.g. flyers, posters, banners*):


Production in alternative formats (*e.g. large type, cassette versions, translations*):


Distribution costs (*e.g. mail or deliver to display sites*):


Recording costs (*for public service announcements*):


Promotional event costs (*e.g. theme party, author signing*):


Promotional give-aways (*e.g. balloons, bookmarks*):


Displays:


Operational expenses (*including telephone, postage, office supplies*):


Other:

## PROGRAM COSTS

Program coordinator and others salaries (*note positions, % of work time to be devoted to project, annual salary including fringe benefits*):

Honoraria for scholars, performers, and/or discussion leaders (*note number of hours or days, fee per hour or day*):

Travel reimbursements (*may include personal car mileage, train or airfare, lodging, meals*):

Space rental:

Books or other reading materials (*note number of volumes to be purchased and average cost per volume including tax if applicable*):

Photocopying of handout materials (*e.g. bibliographies, locally created readers*):

Production of handouts in alternative formats (*e.g. large type, cassette versions, translations*):

Production of original media:

Rentals of exhibits, videos, or other program components:

Production of exhibit text in alternative formats (*e.g. large type, cassette versions, translations*):

Delivery, assembly, insurance for exhibits:

Rental of AV and other equipment etc. for performances:

Fees for sign language interpreters, translators, etc. for performances:

Refreshments:

Operational expenses (*including telephone, postage, office supplies*):

Other:

# EVALUATION COSTS

Program coordinator and others salaries (*note positions, % of work time to be devoted to project, annual salary including fringe benefits*):

Evaluator salary:

Photocopying or printing of evaluation forms:

Production of evaluation forms in alternative formats (*e.g. large type, cassette versions, translations*):

Film and developing charges (*if photographs are part of your evaluation/reporting plans*):

Statistical analysis of evaluations:

Photocopying or printing of final report:

Production of report in alternative formats (*e.g. large type, cassette versions, translations*):

Operational expenses (*including telephone, postage, office supplies*):

## KEEPING TRACK OF EXPENSES

### Expense Documentation

Each library and collaborating agency will have its own method of tracking expenses. As soon as you know that the project will really happen, you should make an appointment with the business manager to learn the requirements for financial reporting. There is no need to reinvent the wheel and develop your own system unless the funding agency requires separate reports which the business office cannot complete for you, or there will be no separate account for the program. In either of those cases you may want to keep track yourself, both so you can report to the funder and so you will know next time exactly what the program *did* cost. Writing your next budget will be significantly easier with some real figures at hand.

Of course expenses can be tracked via computer using spreadsheet or other software. But for those libraries (and librarians) which are not automated, a pen and ink form follows.

## ITEMIZED EXPENDITURES FOR XYZ HUMANITIES PROGRAM

*Month:*

| Budget Category | Cash Outlay | In-Kind Reported | Total |
|---|---|---|---|

*Personnel - Salaries & Honoraria*

   1.

   2.

   3.

   4.

   5.

   6.

*Travel*

   1.

   2.

   3.

*Books and Other Library Materials*

   1.

   2.

   3.

   4.

   5.

   6.

*Video or other media rentals*

*Operating Expenses*
 *Telephone*
 *Postage*
 *Courier Services*
 *Office Supplies*
 *Photocopying*
 *Fiscal Agent*

*Equipment Rental*

*Space Rental*

*Exhibits*
 *Rental*
 *Shipping*
 *Installation*
 *Insurance*

*Promotion*
 *Graphic Artist*
 *Recording*
 *Printing*
 *Distribution*
 *Purchase of Items*

*Refreshments*

*Other*

One typical expense is travel expense or mileage reimbursement for scholars, performers, and discussion leaders. The library reimburses these individuals for their personal outlay for items such as use of a personal car (which includes gasoline and wear and tear) or train tickets. Each person who may submit for reimbursement should be given a form to use. Here is a sample:

---

# TRAVEL REIMBURSEMENT FOR XYZ HUMANITIES PROGRAM

Name:

Title:

Address:

Telephone number:

| Travel to/from | Purpose | Date | Total Miles | Tolls, Parking, etc. |
|---|---|---|---|---|
| | | | | |

Total Miles:

*Note: Reimbursement will be calculated at ___ cents per mile.*

| Travel to/from | Purpose | Date | Plane/Train Ticket | Other Expenses |
|---|---|---|---|---|
| | | | | |

*Note: Other expenses include airport/station transfer, hotel and meals. The limit on such expenses per day is ____.*

Signature:
Date:

---

### In-Kind Documentation

Each individual or agency which donates in-kind staff time, supplies, equipment, or space should keep a contribution log, to be submitted to the program coordinator on a set schedule. Your library may want these records to be collected monthly, or may prefer to receive them only upon completion of the project. In order to make the logs easy for others to use and easy for you (or other library staff) to compile, you should create simple forms and require their use. Here are samples of forms for an agency (e.g. a partner) and a one-time contribution by an individual (e.g. scholar):

# IN-KIND CONTRIBUTIONS TO THE XYZ HUMANITIES PROGRAM

Agency/Organization Contributing:

Person completing form:

Contact Phone Number:

Time Period Covered:

| Date | Type of Services/Items | Number of Hours | Items | Estimated Value Per Hr/Item | Total |
|------|------------------------|-----------------|-------|-----------------------------|-------|
| 1. | | | | | |
| 2. | | | | | |
| 3. | | | | | |
| 4. | | | | | |
| 5. | | | | | |
| 6. | | | | | |
| 7. | | | | | |
| 8. | | | | | |
| 9. | | | | | |
| 10 | | | | | |
| 11. | | | | | |
| 12. | | | | | |
| | *Totals:* | | | | |

I certify that the above figures reflect the contributions made by my agency to the XYZ Humanities Program. The total value of the contributions is estimated to be:

Signed: _____ Date: _____

# IN-KIND CONTRIBUTIONS TO THE XYZ HUMANITIES PROGRAM

Individual Contributing:

Role:

Contact Phone Number:

Time Period Covered:

Date of service or contribution:

Type of service or item:

Number of hours of service:

Fair market value of services or items contributed:

Signature:                                          Title:

Social Security Number:                    Date:

# 4 BUILDING AN AUDIENCE

As Patricia Hurd and Jordy Vantresca write about their poetry programs in Ohio, the "key ingredient [was] a group of people who were hungry for the experience of listening, thinking, and learning together. Finding those people and providing a setting that would meet that need for intellectual growth was the real challenge of the program. They found us, and they came. In doing so, they helped us fulfill our mission to make the library a true center of life-long learning."

Americans enjoy humanities activities. According to the 1993 survey on the importance of arts and humanities, 89% of the public report that they spent time during the previous year discussing history, philosophy, politics, and religion; 87% read for pleasure; nearly half (46%) visited a museum or art gallery, and 31% wrote poetry or fiction for pleasure (National Cultural Alliances, pp. 4–8).

So humanities events are popular and you know you have a great program idea. But how will you find participants? Usually, the efforts to ensure participation in a program are called "publicity" or "public relations," but building an audience is more than that and must begin before any specific program is designed.

## THE GROUNDWORK

The library must develop a climate for humanities programs, have a reputation for holding interesting events, and be in tune with the community.

First, the library must develop a *climate* for humanities programs. The library must be a familiar and friendly place, where people in the community feel comfortable both with staff and with books. You can set up such expectations many ways. Beef up your readers' advisory services so that readers have a more personal relationship with staff. Devote a public bulletin board to information on local cultural events. Do books displays related to holidays, Banned Book Week, and National Library Week. Hand out bibliographies and bookmark book lists.

Next, the library must have a *reputation* for holding interesting programs and events. The library should be a place where people turn for the introduction and discussion of books and ideas. Once you have done a few programs word will spread and you will find a core audience that will not only attend, but spread the word to others. You can develop a reputation before producing your first program by co-sponsoring events with other arts or humanities agencies or with community organizations. If possible, encourage other groups to use the library meeting room for their lectures, symposia, shows, and discussions.

Finally, the library must be *in tune with the community*. To be sure you are, involve your users in developing programs. Include patrons on the planning committee. Do a simple survey of your regular users' interests. Or have a community meeting on the possibilities of humanities programming in the library. Ask patrons to sign up if they want to be informed of future programs. All of the information gathered these ways can assist in the planning of programs, the forecasting of attendance numbers, and future publicity. This is another area in which community collaboration pays off; one or more of your partner agencies may already have a built-in audience for a program like yours. The Southern Connecticut Library Council reports that members of co-sponsoring groups comprised 22% of the audiences at their "American Lives" series in thirty libraries.

Note that most programs attract a mainstream audience. In the national *Let's Talk About It* pilot program, the average participant was a white, middle-aged, well-educated female. 82% of participants were female and 64% were 36–65 years old. 90% of participants were white despite the inclusion of fourteen diverse states. And 87% had attended college with 68% having had some graduate school education (Rubin and Durrance, pp. 3–4). Since then, programmers have worked harder to include people of different ethnicities, ages, and educational level in humanities programs, and many have been successful. Creating such diversity is still difficult, but well worth the trouble because of the added richness to discussion and the important modeling of multicultural exchange. To encourage participation by many different types of people, the library must be seen as valuable, the content must be relevant, and the publicity must be targeted appropriately.

All library programmers warn novices that some programs just never have a large attendance. Despite every effort at building an audience and promoting a specific program, most librarians have a personal horror story or two about the time only three people showed up. Sometimes the reason was an esoteric topic or a little known author, sometimes unexpected bad weather, or a calendar conflict with a popular event. If the program has been carefully planned, in collaboration with other organizations and agencies in the community, the number of "rained out" programs should be minimal.

Sylvia Riggs Liroff, manager of the National Council on the Aging's *Discovery Through the Humanities* program cautions programmers against worrying too much about group size. Some-

> To encourage participation by many different types of people, the library must be seen as valuable, the content must be relevant, and the publicity must be targeted appropriately.

Most humanities programs work best with a moderate-sized group. Thoughtful discussion and interplay among the speaker/performer and the audience are nearly impossible with a large crowd.

times the group will grow through word of mouth. She advises "Begin with a group of enthusiastic participants known to you, or begin off-site where such a group already exists."

Remember, too, that most humanities programs work best with a moderate-sized group. Thoughtful discussion, and interplay *among* the speaker/performer and the audience are nearly impossible with a large crowd. To be sure that you do not have too large a group, you may want to ask people to sign up ahead of time because of a size limit. As one veteran programmer reports "We found registration (at the library or by call-in) to be very helpful. . . . Signing their name seems to bring stronger commitment to attending and limiting the number tends to persuade a person to sign up quickly (come to a decision earlier) and makes them feel part of a 'select' group." An added benefit of asking people to register is that you will know beforehand if you are likely to have too few attendees; with that information you can step up the intensity of your publicity. And the registration lists can come in handy when preparing your next program.

The bottom line is that a good public relations campaign increases the community's overall awareness of the library. One of the most valuable side effects of mounting a humanities program is increased interest in all of the library's services and resources. In other words, by promoting your new humanities program, you are building an audience for the library as a whole. Note too that, by building the community's expectations of the library, you are laying the groundwork for public support—in terms of ballot measures, funding, volunteers—that you may need at another time.

By building the community's expectations of the library, you are laying the groundwork for public support that you may need at another time.

## BEFORE THE PROGRAMS

### PLANNING THE PUBLICITY

About six months prior to your first program, it is time to begin planning your publicity. This is not something you should, or can, do alone. Convening a public relations committee, perhaps a sub-committee of the project advisory committee, is a good approach. This group should discuss the following questions:

- Who do you want to attract? Out-of-school adults, for sure. With an emphasis on what? Male or female? Certain ethnic groups? Non-library users? Recent graduates? Older adults? New readers?

- Where can these people be found? Be sure to think of places outside the library itself: local restaurants and hangouts, service and religious organizations, social and recreational groups, cultural groups, professional organizations.
- How can these people best be reached? Presentations to the groups identified above? Flyers inserted in other mailings? Posters, placemats, displays? Radio or TV spots? Electronic bulletin boards and listservs? Newspapers? Don't forget in-house displays and handouts in the library too.
- How do you answer the basic question of potential participants: "What's in it for me?" Why would someone want to come? Intellectual stimulation, interpersonal contact, personal growth, enjoyment?
- What message do you want to send? Funny or serious? Down-home or sophisticated? Do you want a logo or an identifiable typeface?
- Who should do the publicity? Include advisory committee members—remember that they were chosen to represent certain groups in the community and are obvious ambassadors. Also include Friends of the Library members, board members, and staff.

The publicity committee should develop a publicity plan detailing who is responsible for what and when. See sample plan below.

# SAMPLE PUBLICITY PLAN

Name and position of person responsible for program publicity:

Others on publicity committee and their responsibilities:

How library staff will be kept informed (include when and by whom for each effort):

In-library publicity:

Co-sponsoring organizations, agencies, businesses:

Newsletters for each of the above:

Local newspapers to receive press releases (include when and by whom):

Local radio and/or TV stations to receive press releases and/or public service announcements (include when and by whom):

Radio shows and newspaper reporters to contact re interviews or articles (include when and by whom):

Publicity materials to be sent to the following groups, agencies, businesses (include when and by whom):

Publicity materials to be sent to the following neighboring libraries (include when and by whom):

Publicity materials to be posted where (include when and by whom):

Influential people to contact personally about the program (include when and by whom):

Community groups to contact to arrange a presentation about the program (include when and by whom):

## BASICS OF PUBLICITY

Your publicity must answer these basic five questions and their corollaries:

- Who? Who are the speakers? Who are the sponsors? Who are the contact people at the library? Who should attend?
- What? What is the program? What will happen at the program? What is expected of participants?
- Where? Where will the program be held? Where is the closest transportation or parking?
- When? Date? Starting and ending times? When will it be repeated?
- Why? Why is the library doing this? Why would someone want to attend?

Ideally, the public will see or hear the answers to these questions at least three different times.

## TYPES OF PUBLICITY

The most common publicity approaches are personal contact, written materials, graphics, broadcast media, displays, and advertising items. Most programmers use a combination of these. A study of the first fourteen states *Let's Talk About It* programs were held in found that the most frequently used forms of publicity were, in descending order, displays and posters in the library, news releases, informing community leaders, and radio announcements. These forms were used by 53% to 96% of the libraries. Less than half of the libraries posted flyers outside of the library, spoke to community groups, purchased newspaper advertising, or produced TV public service announcements (Durrance).

Respondents to the 1995 survey report that publicity items which are less common than flyers and posters reach new people and get the community talking about the library. For example, a number of libraries rave about tent signs or placemats in local restaurants, including fast food chains. One librarian who took this approach in a rural county reports: "Many people who see that publicity will never come but they are always commenting to us 'The library does so much; there's always something going on.'"

In addition to restaurants, think about stores which attract the "humanities kind of people." What about book stores, record stores, video rental outlets? These are good locations for posters or flyers, and such businesses may also be willing to co-sponsor.

The bottom line is that a good public relations campaign increases the community's overall awareness of the library.

Andrea Lapsley, Director of Marketing and Development at the Houston Public Library (TX), states that over fifty percent of her library programs' participants report having heard about the program from print publicity (Lapsley).

For the other forty plus percent of people, personal contact is considered most effective. Letters can be mailed to individuals with an interest in the topic (e.g. a reader known to the reference staff), to people who may influence others to come (e.g. English teachers) and to people who have participated in similar events before. Many libraries report that they ask participants to sign in at each session and the library then compiles a mailing list. Judith Cooper, Development and Program Officer at the Prince Georges County Memorial Library System (MD) reports that she has compiled a list of over 4,000 African American residents who have attended library programs during the past five years. Carefully placed telephone calls can convince people who have been only considering attending. Remember that these letters and phone calls can be from library board members, advisory committee members, friends of the libraries, and other people besides the program coordinator. And be persistent—repeated communications pay off.

Another personal approach is to make presentations to local groups. Presentations both attract attendees and help spread the word in the community. Committee members who have the contacts and/or belong to the organizations you want to reach are perfect candidates to give the talks; you may want to provide them with an outline of key points and essential facts.

There are many excellent resources for information on the actual production of written materials, graphics, displays, and broadcast pieces (including public service announcements or PSAs). With the advent of desk top publishing, this is easier than ever to do. One good resource is *Full Time Public Relations with Full Time Results: A PR Primer for Public Libraries* by Rashelle S. Karp (American Library Association, 1995). However, if you feel unprepared to take this on, recruit graphic artists or advertising firms to assist you so that the materials are attractive and professional.

Basically you want all your promotional materials to be catchy, informative, enthusiastic, and accessible. As for that last item, always produce some publicity in large type and in whatever languages are spoken in your community. Under the Americans with Disabilities Act, libraries are required to include people with disabilities in all programs and services and to make informational materials accessible.

In planning publicity, remember that your local newspaper(s) can be a great ally. Many programmers recommend establishing rapport with the newspaper ahead of time, perhaps including a representative on the planning committee. If you can find a media co-sponsor for your program, you can avoid cash outlays for publicity or (often) for printing.

Although the press release is the basic form of information for the print and broadcast media, you will also want to approach the media in other ways. Submit a listing for the events calendars. Arrange a feature story; many library programmers have found that the paper will do an article if there is a human interest story involved. If you are using scholars in the program, ask them to be interviewed. Is one of the authors to be discussed a local person? That's always an angle to try for a feature story. The Vermont Center for the Book has been successful in having scholars write Op-Ed pieces for local papers.

Because not everyone reads the newspaper—especially people who are adult new readers or who are print handicapped—replicate the material in audio form for radio use. All radio stations have some time each week devoted to local spots as well as a time allotment for public service announcements (PSAs). These should be submitted to the station about six weeks before a program; then follow up with a personal contact.

Jean Shrier of the Peoria (IL) Public Library reports that they have had good luck using drive time talk radio for publicity. And Kate Oser of the Southern Connecticut Library Council recommends cable TV for both PSAs and interviews with scholars and authors.

Don't underestimate the library's own promotional vehicles. Although it is important to advertise outside the library, displays inside the library and notices in the library's newsletters are sure-fire ways to reach current users. Does your library have a marquee? If not, how about hanging a banner in front of the building? Do you already have a mailing list of patrons or some of them (e.g. Friends members, donors, people whose children have attended story hours)? Send out a targeted mailing to these people and set up in-house displays a month ahead of the first program. One other in-house resource is invaluable: the staff. Be sure that they know about the program and can "talk it up" and answer questions about it.

Besides the library's newsletter, place articles in the newsletters of your partner agencies and organizations and your business sponsors. Contact other groups around town which do regular mailings—can a flyer for your program be included? Is there a calendar on which your program can be listed? Will the high school principal mention it in the school newsletter? What other sources of free publicity can you find?

If all of the above "basic" promotional activities are not enough—if you feel that public response is lacking and registration is low—you may want to mount some special events to attract additional attention. Libraries have had author readings, art contests, radio programs, theme parties, reading by local celebrities such as the mayor, costume contests, and other events to publicize a new program series. People who come to the events are likely to attend the programs, and in covering the event, the media promotes the program as well. The problem with events of this nature is that they take a great deal of human and other resources which you may need to hold in check for the programs themselves.

## DURING THE PROGRAM SERIES

Publicity should not stop before the first program. Because of natural attrition, you must continually refresh the audience with new attendees as well as reminding people who are already coming. So continue posting flyers, distributing bookmarks, airing PSAs, and making presentations. Send reminder cards to participants—this is important to counteract the attendance attrition which most program series experience. And because word of mouth is so powerful, encourage everyone at the program to tell others about it, too.

Immediately after the first program send out a press release about the success of the event with photographs if possible; include information about the next program. Submit the calendar listing for the next program to the paper(s) and radio station(s). Arrange for a media interview with participants and presenters.

## PROMOTION CALENDAR

Six Months Prior to Program:
- Convene promotion committee. Develop strategy and assign responsibilities. Write a publicity plan (sample above).

Three Months Prior:
- Check local media's deadlines and adapt this calendar to your own situation.

- Call program chairs of community groups to schedule presentations to be given next month.
- Prepare artwork for graphics.
- Develop a fact sheet about the program.

Two Months Prior :
- Contact radio and TV public service directors to arrange PSAs.
- Contact producers of radio and TV community affairs shows, and editors of community newspaper pages, to arrange coverage.
- Submit media calendar listings.
- Explain program to all library staff.
- Arrange for notices in the library's own newsletter.
- Direct mail to potential participants and to influential residents.

One Month Prior:
- Print fliers and other promotional pieces. Post around town.
- Contact media again.
- Write press releases.
- Mount an in-library display about the program.
- Letters of invitation to potential participants and to influential residents.

Two Weeks Prior:
- Submit press releases.
- Telephone contacts to community leaders.
- Presentations at local organizations.

One Week Prior:
- Contact news media to encourage editors to assign a reporter to the first program.

Day of First Program:
- Double-check with local media to confirm coverage.

Immediately Following First Program:
- Write and submit a press release about the program.
- Submit calendar listings for next program.
- Send reminder cards to participants.

After Last Program:
- Write a letter to newspaper editor thanking participants and volunteers.

# 5 MANAGING AND EVALUATING PROGRAM

## MANAGING THE ONGOING PROGRAM

In addition to planning and preparing for the programs, management includes program tasks both during and immediately after the individual events. The coordinator's responsibilities the day of the program include attending the programs themselves, making introductions, and circulating among the participants.

Of the fifty-two project coordinators who responded to the survey, twenty (38%) found these assignments the most fun of all. As one librarian put it "*This* is the pay-off for me. *This* is how I become renewed in my commitment to programming. If participation is 'managing the programs,' then this is my favorite activity." Another wrote "Attending the programs is *always* the best part—seeing the fruits of our labors, the values of these programs, and the *real* people who get so much out of them!" A third said "I *love* attending the programs. It reminds me each time *why* I do all the other stuff."

### DURING THE PROGRAM SERIES

Managing the ongoing program is a combination of last minute details and pure enjoyment. In the former category are:

- paying scholars and discussion leaders
- preparing the meeting room
- checking in with the media
- following through on publicity
- keeping copies of all publicity
- preparing and compiling evaluations
- trouble shooting as necessary
- reminding participants of next program (postcards? bookmarks?)

The other group of activities are fun and rewarding because they involve attending the program:

- welcoming the participants
- introducing scholars and discussion leaders

- monitoring attendance
- acting as timekeeper
- closing the program (including public thank yous)

Below are two checklists for your use. One is for the opening night and the other is for the day after the program is completed.

---

# OPENING NIGHT CHECKLIST

*Facilities*

_____ Signs directing participants to meeting room?

_____ Room set-up completed?

_____ Enough chairs? Arranged in circle or horseshoe?

_____ Clock?

_____ Water?

_____ Coatrack?

_____ Audiovisual equipment as needed? Checked for power supply, bulbs, etc.?

_____ Attendance sheet?

_____ Name tags?

_____ Book or other displays?

_____ Refreshments ready?

_____ Evaluation forms?

*Human Resources*

_____ Scholar and discussion leaders ready?

_____ Introductions of them written?

_____ Their paychecks ready?

_____ Any volunteers set?

_____ Media on the way?

---

Managing the program is a combination of last minute details and pure enjoyment.

## UPON COMPLETION OF THE PROGRAM

After the program (or program series) is over, the inevitable paperwork awaits. Your immediate business includes:

- thank you notes to all collaborating agencies
- thank you notes to all planning committee members
- thank you notes to all library staff who helped
- thank you notes to all scholars and discussion leaders
- thank you notes to any reporters or editors who gave exceptional coverage
- thank you notes to any business sponsors (e.g. the bookstore)
- compilation and analysis of all evaluation forms
- payment of all outstanding bills
- compilation of all in-kind contributions
- compilation of all attendance lists
- final report—to funding agency as required, to advisory committee members, to library administration—based on all the above pieces

Though it may be tempting to skimp on these tasks—after all, the program you've been planning for a year is finally over and you've earned a vacation—don't let yourself. These activities ensure that when you are ready to do another program that you will have co-sponsors, individuals, scholars, media representatives, funding agencies, and co-workers all on your side.

# EVALUATION

The best evaluation grows directly from planning; planning develops the objectives which are measured in evaluation.

Imagine a moebius strip—a ribbon of paper, twisted once and attached seamlessly so that it is forever continuous. Planning and evaluation of your program are two points on the strip. In other words, evaluation is inseparable from planning. The best planning is based on the lessons learned from experience; evaluation is the methodology for collecting and understanding those lessons. The best evaluation grows directly from planning; planning develops the objectives which are measured in evaluation.

Evaluation is also like a mirror—it only reflects what is put in front of it.

Evaluation is also like a mirror—it only reflects what is put in front of it. If you want to reflect the enthusiasm of the discussion, collecting data on zip codes is not helpful. You must decide *why* you want to evaluate so you can decide *what* to evaluate. In other words, are you evaluating to fulfill the requirements of a funding source? If so, what are they most interested in? Numbers of participants or quality of presentation? Are you assessing the program to find out which groups in your community did and did not attend? To improve your future planning? It is essential to think through the purposes of your evaluation so you do not collect information you do not need: the most common mistake new evaluators make is to do work which is ultimately unnecessary.

Analogies aside, evaluation is also a set of activities which you, the program coordinator, are responsible for. None of the survey respondents selected evaluation as their favorite activity. Tim McGorey of the Monroe County Library System (MI) summarized all the comments. "Evaluation is part of the process when the thrill is diminishing." Certainly evaluation isn't as much fun as attending a program, but it can yield information which will make you feel good—and help you with your next program.

Before jumping into the how of collecting the information on which evaluations are based, consider the following possible approaches:

- Subjective appraisals by participants and scholars as to whether their own objectives (e.g. learning about poetry, meeting others interested in history, sharing ideas with out-of-school adults) were met.
- Subjective measures by program staff, other library staff members, and collaborating agencies as to whether your objectives (e.g. to attract new users to the library, to increase circulation of non-fiction, to work cooperatively with the parks and recreation department) were met.
- Objective assessment (by a neutral person) of the cost-effectiveness of the program (e.g. expenditures and staff time balanced against the program's value). This may be required by your funding agency.
- Objective judgment (by an outside evaluator) of the humanities content of the program. This may be required if a humanities council is involved in funding or sponsoring your program.
- Analysis of an unsuccessful program (e.g. why did so few people come? Was it the topic or the publicity or the meeting time?)

Most program coordinators use a combination of these approaches because each offers a different set of "lessons" which can be used to improve the next attempts, attract financial support and community partners, and publicize future programs.

Oral self-reports, interviews, and written surveys are the most common forms of program evaluation. Anecdotal pieces, such as oral self-reports, often provide the "warm, fuzzy" kind of comments that coordinators, planning committees, and funders love to hear. For example, "This was the best discussion I've ever been in." Interviews yield similar remarks and can be useful to elicit remarks from people who will not spontaneously comment. But interviews are labor-intensive and, because they are not anonymous, often do not bring out criticisms. Therefore, written surveys are the most frequently used evaluation tool.

If, however, your intended audience members use English as a second language, are adult new readers, have disabilities, or are otherwise uncomfortable with written/printed forms, you may have to provide the survey in another language or format, or arrange for oral interviews.

Included here are sample evaluation forms for participants, planning committee members, discussion leaders, scholars, and program coordinator (you). But before you use them wholesale, consider adapting them to your specific situation.

- Are you doing a series? If so, you may want to evaluate after the first session so you can make changes to improve the program. The last session is too late. You may also want to evaluate the first and second sessions to see if your changes had the desired effect.
- Are you hoping to repeat the program? If so, you will want feedback on the specific components of the program such as the readings, the placement of the exhibit, the effectiveness of the speaker.
- Are you planning to do other programs? If so, you may want to add questions about the arrangements to know if you should make changes in the location, times, duration, etc. If it is a discussion program, you may want to ask more detailed questions on the structure such as discussion group size, lecture length, discussion group length. And you will want to ask about other topics of interest.
- Are you attempting to reach new audiences? If so, you may want to ask about prior library use and previous discussion group experience. You might also want additional demographic information such as educational level, age, zip code, etc. And you will want to ask about publicity: how did you hear about the program? Where else should we publicize future programs?

Note that the sample forms include a mixture of open-ended questions and scaled responses. Some people are more comfortable with one style of survey than another, and including both types of questions ensures that everyone will answer something. Also some questions are more suited to one type of question than another. Asking for "other comments" is important both because someone may have an answer to a question you neglected to ask, and because that blank space elicits the written equivalent to an oral self-report.

These sample forms are based on *Let's Talk About It* and assume that the program includes reading (and/or viewing or hearing) followed by a scholar's lecture and a discussion. You will need to modify the forms based on your own program's structure.

A last word on evaluation from Debbie Spear, full-time library programmer at the Greenville County Library (SC): "Remember that you can't always judge the 'success' of a program immediately based on numbers or anything else. Humanities programming often sparks unexpected results somewhere *way* down the road for unlikely people in unlikely places."

"Remember that you can't always judge the success of a program immediately."

## SAMPLE EVALUATION FORM FOR PARTICIPANT IN DISCUSSION PROGRAM

Please answer the following questions to help us plan future programs. All answers are anonymous.

1. What attracted you to this program? (You can select more than one) topic book (film, performance) format scholar discussion location

2. Was the book (film, performance) the right choice for today's program? Why or why not?

3. To what extent did the lecture (exhibit, performance) enrich your understanding of the book (film, exhibit)? "1" means "not at all" and "5" means "very much."

    1 2 3 4 5

4. To what extent did the lecture (exhibit, performance) enhance your participation in the discussion? "1" means "not at all" and "5" means "very much."

    1 2 3 4 5

5. How successful was your group discussion? "1" means "inadequate" and "5" means "excellent."

    1 2 3 4 5

6. How effective was your discussion leader at facilitating discussion? "1" means "inadequate" and "5" means "excellent."

    1 2 3 4 5

7. Do you plan to attend other programs in this series? Why or why not?

8. Other comments:

## SAMPLE EVALUATION FORM FOR SCHOLAR IN DISCUSSION PROGRAM

1. Was the book (film, performance) the right choice for today's program? Why or why not?

2. Did the program format work well for you?

3. How closely related to the topic was the group discussion? "1" means "not at all" and "5" means "very much."

    1 2 3 4 5

4. How successful were the group discussions? "1" means "inadequate" and "5" means "excellent."

    1 2 3 4 5

5. Please comment on the quality of the humanities experience created by this program:

6. Was there anything else the program coordinator could have done to assist you before the program?

7. Other comments:

## SAMPLE EVALUATION FORM FOR DISCUSSION LEADER IN DISCUSSION PROGRAM

1. Was the book (film, performance) the right choice for today's program? Why or why not?

2. How closely related to the topic was the group discussion ? "1" means "not at all" and "5" means "very much."

   1 2 3 4 5

3. To what extent did the lecture (exhibit, performance) enrich your understanding of the book (film, exhibit)? "1" means "not at all" and "5" means "very much."

   1 2 3 4 5

4. How successful was your group's discussion? "1" means "inadequate" and "5" means "excellent."

   1 2 3 4 5

5. Please comment on the overall quality of the program:

6. Was there anything else the program coordinator or scholar could have done to assist you before the program?

7. Other comments:

## SAMPLE EVALUATION FORM FOR THE PLANNING COMMITTEE

1. What was your (your agency's) main objective for this program?

2. How well was this objective met? "1" means "inadequately" and "5" means "excellently."

   1 2 3 4 5

3. Please comment on the overall quality of the program:

4. Was there anything the committee could have done earlier to improve the program? If so, what?

5. Is there anything the committee can do now to improve subsequent programs? If so, what?

6. Other comments:

# SAMPLE EVALUATION FORM FOR PROGRAM COORDINATOR FOR DISCUSSION PROGRAM

1. How many participants attended?

2. Demographically, how did it look? Did age, sex, or ethnicity distinguish the audience?

3. Do you feel that you reached your intended audience?

4. Had the participants done the reading? If not, why? (e.g. difficulty getting book, difficulty understanding book)

5. How was the book (film, performance) received? (Was it perceived as interesting, difficult, unusual, etc.)

6. How was the lecture received?

7. Describe your impression of the scholar's performance:

8. How successful were the discussion groups? (from unsuccessful to very successful)

9. Describe the participation (e.g. sluggish, enthusiastic, fiery):

10. Were there obvious characteristics which distinguished more successful groups from less successful ones? (e.g. leader talked more or less, group size)

11. Was there an appropriate division of labor among you, scholar, discussion leaders, committee members, other staff?

12. Were there any surprises (positive and/or negative)?

13. What else could others have done to ensure a successful program?

14. What should be changed before another program is presented? (e.g. selection of scholar, training of discussion leaders, publicity, room arrangement)

# 6 NATIONAL PROGRAM PACKAGES

## READING AND DISCUSSION PROGRAMS

### GREAT BOOKS

Great Books is the best known nationally-sponsored book discussion program. Begun in 1945, it was not the first such series (ALA developed *Classics of the Western World* in 1927) but is the largest, continuously vigorous program by far. In 1947 the Great Books Foundation, an independent, non-profit educational corporation, was funded to administer the program. It has its own book series—three for youth and five for adults—published exclusively by the Foundation, which describes them as "collections of excellent literature." Each of the adult series includes fifteen readings, fiction and non-fiction, excerpts and full works, classic and "modern" (but none by contemporary authors). Participants meet for discussion with a leader trained in book discussion by the Foundation, which trains 17,000 leaders each year. As the Foundation describes the program, "Central to all Great Books programs is a method of interpretive reading and discussion called shared inquiry. In shared inquiry, participants and discussion leaders work together to answer questions about important problems of meaning in a challenging text. Guided by the leader's questions, participants develop their own interpretations and support them with reasons and evidence from the text" (Great Books Foundation). For more information, contact the Great Books Foundation (see *Resources*).

### LET'S TALK ABOUT IT

In 1983, the American Library Association was awarded a $1.5 million grant from the National Endowment for the Humanities to promote the development of reading and discussion programs nationwide. Because of its national scope, and because of the NEH funding, *Let's Talk About It* changed the landscape of library-based reading and discussion programs in a number of ways. First, it convened national advisory committees which produced reading lists on carefully selected themes which were then made available to libraries; local libraries no longer had to create their own programs. Second, it provided participating libraries with training, technical assistance, and promotional materials, so that novice libraries could run successful programs. Third, it selected a broad cross-section of libraries for the initial participants so that urban, rural, large and small libraries were all pursuing reading and discussion programs on the same themes. By the end of the original funding in 1987, more than 30,000 adults in 300 public libraries had participated.

*Let's Talk About It* also changed the method and goals of reading and discussion groups, most of which were based on the *Great Books* approach. First, the *Let's Talk About It* model added to the traditional librarian/participant/discussion leader partnership a new member: a humanities scholar whose charge it was to interpret the readings in an oral presentation and provide a humanities context for the discussion. Next, the reading materials mixed old and new, with many contemporary authors included to represent the American spectrum of ethnicity, gender, and politics. Finally, while the discussion centered on the text, it was expected to have two other equally valid bases: the scholar's presentation and the participants' own life experiences.

Originally, *Let's Talk About It* had six themes, used in 168 libraries in fifteen states. The topics were:

- *Making a Living, Making a Life: Work and Its Rewards in a Changing America*
- *The Way We Were, The Way We Are: Seasons in the Contemporary American Family*
- *What America Reads: Myth Making in Popular Fiction*
- *Not For Children Only*
- *Individual Rights and Community in America*
- *Being Ethnic, Becoming American: Struggle, Successes, Symbols*

From 1984 to 1987, four additional themes were created:

- *Contemporary Japanese Literature*
- *Rebirth of a Nation: Nationalism and the Civil War*
- *The Journey Inward: Women's Autobiography*
- *Destruction or Redemption: Images of Romantic Love*

In 1992, to accompany the quincentennial exhibit *Seeds of Change*, ALA developed four more themes:

- *Seeds of Change: The Encounter that Transformed the World*
- *New American Worlds: Writing the Hemisphere*
- *Isabella's Sisters: Women Creating Worlds*
- *Sovereign Worlds: Native Peoples Reclaim Their Lives and Heritage*

*The Many Realms of King Arthur*, created in 1995 in conjunction with the traveling exhibition on King Arthur sponsored by the ALA, the Newberry Library, and NEH, is the most recent theme.

As of now, several hundred libraries have offered one or more of the fifteen existing themes. In the fall of 1996, a theme on the West and the American Frontier will be unveiled. And in 1997, 25 public libraries in 16 states will begin using *The Nation That Works* a new series developed by the ALA division of Public Programs as part of the NEH *National Conversation on American Pluralism and Values* initiative. This series will include the themes:

- *Work Across the Ages: From Grandparents to Generation X*
- *Gender, Work, and American Values*
- *Race, Ethnicity, and the Workplace*
- *Immigration, Migration, and American Identity*
- *Disappearing Borders: New Technology, the American Workplace and the World*

For information on any of the existing or forthcoming themes, contact the ALA Public Programs department. (See *Resources* for contact information.)

In addition to the national *Let's Talk About It* program, a number of local, state and regional *Let's Talk About It* programs have been developed during the past ten years, each with its own theme(s) and reading list(s). Examples include:

- *Seeking Common Ground* The Book Group (Salt Lake City, UT)
- *Morality and the Muse: Ethics in Literature* Howard County Library (MD)
- *American Lives* Southern Connecticut Library Council
- *Landings: New Perspectives on Local History* Indiana Humanities Council
- *The American Renaissance* Let's Talk About It Oklahoma
- *Health and Human Values* Pennsylvania Humanities Council

- *A Sense of Place* Georgia Humanities Committee
- *Talking About Vietnam* Peninsula Library System (CA)
- *Native Grounds* Louisiana Library Association
- *West Virginia Voices* Vienna Public Library (WV)
- *Faith Differences, Different Faiths* Let's Talk About It North Carolina
- *Whodunit?* Middlebury Public Library (IN)
- *Science As Literature* Massachusetts Foundation for the Humanities
- *Images of the Future* State Library of Iowa
- *An Unsuitable Job For A Woman* Anderson County Library (SC)
- *Victims, Villains, Sleuths* Oberlin Public Library (OH)
- *Stories to Live By: Health and Medicine in Literature* Kansas Humanities Council
- *Rogues Gallery: The Folks You Love to Hate* Let's Talk About It Delaware
- *Growing Up Chicano/Growing Up Chicana* South Dakota Humanities Council
- *Living Together* Ohio Humanities Council
- *Braided Lives* South Dakota Humanities Council
- *The Storytellers* Wisconsin Humanities Council
- *Fear and Hope* Maine State Library

For more information, contact the Public Programs office of the ALA (see *Resources*) or see the *Model Programs* section of this book.

## DISCOVERY THROUGH THE HUMANITIES

Eighteen reading and discussion programs for older adults have been developed by the National Council on the Aging, Inc. with NEH funding. Designed to elicit discussion by older people, they also work well with intergenerational groups. Each program centers on a large print anthology created especially for the project; some are also available in Spanish and/or on audiocassette. Themes range from *Remembering World War II* to *Immigrant Women in the United States* to *The American Musical Comedy* to *Exploring Values*. For more information, contact the National Council on the Aging (see *Resources*).

## NATIONAL ISSUES FORUM

Funded by the Topsfield Foundation, the *National Issues Forum Institute* annually selects public policy issues for discussion in local community forums. NIF has been convening discussions since 1982. Libraries and other groups who want to sponsor nonpartisan discussion can receive information on setting up the program locally and can purchase issue books, videotapes, and moderator guides. Training sessions and institutes are held for program leaders. Unlike some of the literature-based discussions, *NIF* groups attract many male as well as female participants. The 1996 discussion topics are:

- *Pocketbook Pressures: Who Benefits From Economic Growth*
- *How Can We Be Fair: The Future of Affirmative Action*
- *Mission Uncertain: Reassessing America's Global Role*
- *How Do We Want to Govern America? The Public and Private Role in Doing America's Work*
- *The Troubled American Family: Which Way Out Of the Storm?*

For more information, contact the *National Issues Forum* (see *Resources*).

### CHOICES FOR THE 21ST CENTURY

Modeled on ALA's *Let's Talk About It*, this is a scholar-led reading and discussion program series on public policy. The thrust is to help citizens to make connections between values and public policy and to enable them to trust their opinions rather than those of the experts. It was developed jointly by the OPTIONS program and the Choices for the 21st Century Education Project, both of Brown University, in 1992. The programs were originally offered only in public libraries in Connecticut, but are available in nine states in 1996.

The pre-packaged program includes reading materials, promotional tools, technical assistance, and scholar training, and is available to state or regional agencies and organizations which will coordinate the programs in their area's public libraries. Libraries using the *Choices* program report that it, like *NIF*, is popular with men as well as women. To borrow a short video about the program, or for more information, contact *Choices* (see *Resources*).

# LISTENING/VIEWING, READING AND DISCUSSION PROGRAMS

### POETS IN PERSON

Based on the successful public radio programs, sponsored by the Modern Poetry Association, and funded by the National Endowment for the Humanities, *Poets in Person* is a listening, reading, and discussion program series which has been used by more than seventy libraries. The series comprises thirteen programs, each devoted to one contemporary poet ranging from Allen Ginsberg to Rita Dove. Program materials for each consist of a thirty minute cassette of the poet reading and discussing his/her work and a print Listener's Guide. A Planner's Manual is also available.

Some libraries have developed themes and chosen poetry from the *Poets In Person* series that relates to it. For example, the Medina (OH) Library created "Weather of the Heart," using five of the poets. A scholar presentation on the theme (rather than on a specific poet) plus discussion equals a new and different discussion series.

For more information, contact the Modern Poetry Association (see *Resources*).

## VOICES AND VISIONS

A joint effort by the Annenberg/Corporation for Public Broadcasting and the American Library Association, *Voices and Visions* is a viewing, reading and discussion program series which has been used by more than one hundred libraries. Using the videos on American poets which were developed for PBS, this program adds a print anthology, pamphlets on each of the thirteen poets, publicity posters, and a programmer's kit. The poets include Emily Dickinson, T.S. Eliot, Langston Hughes, Sylvia Plath, and William Carlos Williams.

Again, libraries may mix and match poets to select poems on a locally developed theme. By adding a scholar presentation on the theme (rather than on a specific poet) and group discussion, a new series is developed using the *Voices and Visions* materials.

For more information, contact the ALA Public Programs Office (see *Resources*).

# LITERACY HUMANITIES PROGRAMS

Although learning to read per se is not a humanities function, "cultural literacy" is. This term, coined by Daniel Boorstin when he was Librarian of Congress, refers to the second stage of literacy. That is, once a person learns the basics of reading, she or he needs to learn how to understand, evaluate, and consider what is read. Humanities programs for adult new readers use low level reading materials for these purposes. The programs are not instructional but serve as an adjunct to literacy training.

## MOTHEREAD

Originally designed for two women's prisons in North Carolina, *Motheread* is an intergenerational reading program for adult new readers and very young readers, their children. Reading themes are chosen for their relevance to the parents who discuss the books in small groups before introducing them to their children at home. Currently, Motheread programs are available in North Carolina, Minnesota, and California where they are now called *Motheread/ Fatheread*.

*Motheread* is a private non-profit family literacy organization. Individual programs are funded by local foundations and the state humanities councils. For more information, contact Narcye Gaj, President, Motheread, 4208 Six Forks Road, Bldg 2, Suite 335, Raleigh, NC 27609. (919) 781–2088.

## NATIONAL ISSUES FORUM

The *National Issues Forum* provides materials for adult new readers so that they can participate in the *NIF* programs described above. Some library-based literacy programs have integrated the *NIF* materials and forum participation into their programs. For example, Project Read at the South San Francisco Public Library (CA) uses *NIF* as a way to break down the isolation which results from illiteracy. For more information, contact *NIF* (see *Resources*) or Leslie Shelton, Director, Project Read, 840 W. Orange Avenue, South San Francisco, CA 94080. (415) 877–5329.

# AUTHOR PROGRAMS

## WRITERS LIVE AT THE LIBRARY

Funded by the Lila Wallace-Reader's Digest Fund, the American Library Association has sponsored *Writers Live* at 29 small public libraries (serving populations of 150,000 or less) in nine Midwestern states since its inception in 1993. The project brings writers to libraries to "increase the visibility of the library as a literary forum." Participating libraries, working in conjunction with a local partner agency, select an author from a national roster. The author then spends a full day at the library as the key event in a year-long series of literary programs. For more information, contact the Public Programs Office of ALA (see *Resources*).

# EXHIBITS

Many libraries are borrowing (or renting) exhibits to be the centerpiece of humanities programming, whether lectures, symposia, or public discussions. Besides the examples described below, a good source of humanities exhibit information is available from the Humanities Exchange which publishes a newsletter, a book, and search software (see *Resources*).

## AMERICAN LIBRARY ASSOCIATION COOPERATIVE EXHIBITS

During the past twelve years, the American Library Association has worked with the New York Public Library, the Newberry Library, the Smithsonian Institution, and Time Warner to develop exhibits.

Since 1984, ALA and the New York Public Library have worked together to develop traveling exhibitions that have toured public libraries. Funded by the National Endowment for the Humanities, these topics were developed:

- *Censorship and Libraries* 1984–1986
- *Are We To Be A Nation* 1987–1988
- *Printing and the French Revolution* 1988–1990
- *New Worlds, Ancient Texts* 1991–1993

From 1995 to 1997, *The Many Realms of King Arthur* has been traveling the United States. This exhibit was created by ALA in cooperation with the Newberry Library in Chicago and funding from the NEH. Note that ALA created a *Let's Talk About It* reading and discussion series to coordinate with this exhibit.

Based upon an exhibit at the National Museum of American History (Smithsonian Institution) and funded by the National Endowment for the Humanities, *A More Perfect Union: Japanese Americans and the United States Constitution* is a traveling exhibit based on photographs, oral histories, recordings, and documents. It is scheduled at twenty library sites through 1998.

In 1996, another traveling exhibit sponsored by ALA in cooperation with the Newberry Library in Chicago, and funded by the National Endowment for the Humanities, will visit thirty public and academic libraries. *The Frontier in American Culture,* through photographs, maps and other pictorial materials, examines how stories and images of settling of the west have shaped American identity and values.

A photographic exhibit currently touring libraries was developed by Time Warner in 1994. In the tradition of the photo essay invented by *Life* magazine, *It's US: A Celebration of Who We Are In America Today* is an exhibit which celebrates "the vibrant tapestry that embodies the meaning and strength of our American way of life."

For more information on any of the above, contact the Public Programs office of ALA (see *Resources*).

## SMITHSONIAN INSTITUTION TRAVELING EXHIBITION SERVICE/ ALA EXHIBITS

With support from the National Endowment for the Humanities, ALA has joined with the Smithsonian Institution Traveling Exhibition Service (SITES) to create the following exhibits for extended tours of public libraries:

- *Seeds of Change* 1991–1993
- *Beyond Category: The Musical Genius of Duke Ellington* 1995–1997

Typically, libraries paid for insurance and onward shipping. Note that ALA also created materials for reading and discussion programs to coordinate with the exhibits. For more information contact the Public Programs office of the ALA (see *Resources*).

## SMITHSONIAN INSTITUTION TRAVELING EXHIBITION SERVICE (SITES)

In addition to the ALA partnership exhibits, SITES develops and circulates many other exhibits. Based on the Smithsonian Institution's collections, often in collaboration with other museums and organizations, SITES exhibits vary in size, cost, and security requirements because many are used by major museums around the country. Recently, though, SITES has been creating smaller, lightweight, free-standing, inexpensive exhibits based on the larger ones, specifically so that libraries, small museums, and schools can provide access to the Smithsonian scholarship. Each exhibit circulates for a limited amount of time before finding a permanent home. In this category, current and upcoming topics include:

- *Saynday Was Coming Along . . . Silverhorn's Drawings of the Kiowa Trickster*
- *Before Freedom Came: African American Life in the Antebellum South*
- *Produce for Victory: Posters on the American Home Front, 1941–1945*
- *Barn Again!*
- *Vanishing Frogs*

Libraries pay a rental fee which includes incoming shipping, insurance, publicity materials, and catalogs. For more information, contact SITES (see *Resources*).

## EXHIBITS USA

A national division of the Mid-America Arts Alliance, Exhibits USA offers exhibits to small and medium-sized libraries and museums. The fifty-one exhibits include sculpture, mixed media, paintings, folk art and crafts, and photography. In 1996, the organization received a large NEH Challenge Grant to improve and expand access to the exhibitions, including keeping the rental prices low. The exhibits vary greatly in cost, size, and security requirements. A sample of themes available:

- *Amazing Graces: Contemporary African American Women Artists*
- *Telling Tales: Children's Book Illustrations*
- *Pure Vision: American Bead Artists*
- *Vision Quest: Men, Women, and Sacred Sites of the Sioux Nation*
- *Fields of Dreams: Architecture and Baseball*

Fees include insurance and incoming shipping, programming workbook, promotional materials, educational materials, and planning workbook. For more information, contact Exhibits USA (see *Resources*).

## LIBRARY OF CONGRESS EXHIBITS

Since 1992, the Library of Congress has offered ten traveling exhibitions which have been seen in ninety libraries, schools, museums and other public spaces in forty states. These exhibits are small, free-standing facsimile presentations which require only limited security. Inspired by the library's collections, the exhibits range widely in topic. Currently touring are:

- *Women Come to the Front: Journalists, Photographers and Broadcasters During World War II*
- *Language of the Land: Journeys into Literary America*
- *The Cultural Landscape of the Plantation (the slaves' side of the plantation)*
- *Paradox of the Press*
- *In Their Own Voices (Native American documents)*
- *Documenting America 1935–43 (the work of twelve photographers)*

Libraries must pay a rental fee which includes incoming shipping, insurance, publicity materials, and educational packet. For more information, contact the Traveling Exhibitions, Interpretive Programs Office of the Library of Congress (see *Resources*).

## SOCIAL ISSUES RESOURCES SERIES/ LIBRARY OF CONGRESS CORNER EXHIBITS

The Social Issues Resources Series (SIRS) and the Library of Congress (LC) have collaborated in developing a subscription series of poster exhibits based on the LC collections. Each exhibit consists of sixteen posters which fit into freestanding display stands. Twelve topics are always available including these current and upcoming ones:

- *Books That Shaped America*
- *"Herstory" and History*
- *The Open Road*
- *The African American Mosaic*
- *Scenes From the Civil War*
- *Many Nations: The Indians and Alaska Native Peoples of the United States*

Libraries may purchase individual displays or order an annual subscription which includes the aluminum display stand and four different exhibits. For more information, contact SIRS (see *Resources*).

## BALCH INSTITUTE FOR ETHNIC STUDIES

The educational wing of the Balch Institute in Philadelphia has developed traveling exhibitions focused on the traditions of ethnic groups in America. The exhibits vary in size, loan period, and security level required. Topics available for under $1,000 include:

- *Something Old, Something New: Ethnic Weddings in America*
- *Ethnic Images in Advertising*
- *Growth of a Dream: The Korean American Experience*
- *Hollywood Reviews the Forward: Photographs By Phil Stern*
- *Interviews: Portraits of Korean Americans*

Libraries pay for round trip shipping in addition to a rental fee which includes insurance. For more information, contact the Balch Institute (see *Resources*).

## TEXAS HUMANITIES RESOURCE CENTER

The Texas Humanities Resource Center (THRC), a division of the Texas Committee for the Humanities, provides traveling exhibits to libraries and others. The exhibits vary greatly in size and cost, though THRC is moving toward smaller, more uniform exhibits. Fifty topics are available including:

- *Istanbul: Portrait of a City*
- *Annexation: The Story of Texas Statehood*
- *The Road to the Promised Land: Martin Luther King, Jr. and the Civil Rights Movement*

Under development are:

- *Cesar Chavez*
- *Latino Literature*

Libraries pay forward shipping and a rental fee based on size of the exhibit and library location. THRC also has catalogs, brochures, discussion guides, bibliographies, promotional materials, and planning guides for each exhibit and related film/video and slide/tape programs for some topics. For more information, contact THRC (see *Resources*).

## BLAIR-MURRAH EXHIBITIONS

Established by a private foundation specifically for the purpose of developing traveling exhibitions, Blair-Murrah creates exhibits from its own collection of source materials. At any one time, approximately seventy-five exhibits are available to school, museums, and libraries. An unusual feature of their exhibits is that Blair-Murrah will customize any exhibit to your space, security arrangements, and financial limits and will provide text and labels in any language. Topics include:

- *Edward S. Curtis: The North American Indian*
- *The Homeless*
- *Valentines: Flattery and Insults*
- *Growing Up Amish: Children and Animals*
- *They Also Ran: Presidential Hopefuls*
- *Kimonos:The Expression of Inner Harmony*

Fees are based on exhibit size and do not include insurance or shipping. For more information, contact Blair-Murrah (see *Resources*).

## SCHOMBURG CENTER FOR RESEARCH IN BLACK CULTURE

The Schomburg Center, one of four research divisions of the New York Public Library, includes a research library, a performing arts venue, and a museum in addition to their traveling exhibition program. Besides their museum-quality traveling exhibits which incorporate original materials, the Schomburg Center has available simpler freestanding exhibits on themes related to black culture. Current topics include:

- *Lady Legends in Jazz*
- *Spiritual Home of Black America: Harlem 1900–1929*
- *New World Africans*

Libraries pay for insurance and shipping in addition to a basic fee which includes brochures. For more information, contact the Traveling Exhibition Program of the Schomburg Center (see *Resources*).

## EXHIBIT TOURING SERVICES

Originally limited to Washington state, Exhibit Touring Services (ETS) now circulates its exhibits nationally. A service of the Eastern Washington University, the exhibits focus primarily, but not exclusively, on pacific northwestern themes.

Although the exhibits are not customized for a specific venue's size, ETS will give advice on which parts of the show to hang, depending on your own size requirements. Current topics include:

- *Glasnost in Cartoons*
- *Portrait of A Racetrack*
- *Ninth National Computer Art Invitational*

For a preview of the pictures, as well as textual information on the exhibits, visit their web page at Http:\\visual.arts.ewu.edu/ets/ets.html. Or contact ETS by mail or phone (see *Resources*).

*Besides these national exhibition services, some individual public libraries have developed exhibits which they will loan. Contact the Public Programs Office at ALA for referrals.*

# 7 MODEL REGIONAL, STATE AND LOCAL PROGRAMS

Programs described in this chapter were selected because of their outstanding qualities. This is not a comprehensive list, however. Fortunately, there are far too many exemplary programs to include them all.

## REGIONAL AND STATE PROGRAMS

**The Book Group: Exploring Literature in Company**

Developing reading and discussion themes, and loaning the materials to libraries, *The Book Group* was founded in 1985 as a Utah project. In 1989, their reading and discussion programs spread to the entire Intermountain Region (Colorado, Wyoming, and Utah). Thirty themes have been developed by *The Book Group* with most of their funding coming from NEH, the Utah Humanities Council, the Utah Arts Council, the Utah Library Association, and the Utah Centennial Commission. Themes include:

- *Trails: Towards a New Western History*
- *Heroes, Heroines and Outlaws: Reimagining the Mythic West*
- *Sacred and Secular: The Human Search for Meaning*
- *Seeking Common Ground*
- *Moments of Truth: Renewing Relationships with East Germany, Czechoslovakia, and Poland*
- *The Restless Spirit*

In 1991 *Human Pursuits: The Western Humanities Concern* was founded to manage the Book Group while fundraising and sponsoring other projects. One of those other projects is *Literature in the Home* which provides resources (including books returned from public programs) to independent, private book groups. Another is *El Lenguaje Que Nos Une/The Language That Unites Us* which develops and implements bilingual reading and discussion programs for the region. These programs may be expanded to Texas and California in the future.

Brochures, press releases, study guides and books are available for rental throughout the US. For more information, contact Helen Cox at Human Pursuits (see *Resources*).

**Connecticut Reading Connections**

Since 1983, the Southern Connecticut Library Council, a regional cooperative library service unit, has sponsored nearly a thousand scholar-led reading and discussion programs. Their current project, begun in 1989, *Connecticut Reading Connections* offers over fifty-five reading and discussion themes in six areas: biography/autobiography, Connecticut and New England literature and history, personal and family relationships, the American experience, other cultures, and genres. Sixty libraries use their "fully-funded and centrally-organized" series and thirty others fund and organize their own series with assistance from CRC. Kate Oser, the director, reports that thirty percent of the CRC programs are home-grown and the rest are imported. CRC developed themes include:

- *The 1960s: Transformations in American Values*
- *The Country and the City: Images in Literature*
- *Evolution of the Detective*
- *Self-Portraits: Autobiographies of American Women*
- *China: Legacy, Literature, and Life after Tianenmen*
- *Private Lives, Public Lives: Exploring American Values Through Biography*

In 1996, an offshoot of *Connecticut Reading Connections* was begun. *Senior Connections*, offered in four Connecticut public libraries, is a scholar-led book discussion group which meets by statewide teleconference. Instead of gathering in the public library, participants in residential facilities will use a speaker phone to communicate with the scholar and other participants. Funded by a Library Services and Construction Act (LSCA) grant from the Connecticut State Library, *Senior Connections* uses *We Got There on the Train: Railroads in the Lives of the American People*, a reader developed by the National Council on Aging's *Discovery Through the Humanities* project.

Although focused on Connecticut, out-of-state libraries may be able to borrow materials. Contact Kate Oser at the Council (see *Resources*).

### Connections (Literacy)

Both New Hampshire and Vermont offer *Connections* programs. Adults and high school students at-risk who read at basic levels meet together in groups for discussion after reading books singly (or with tutors). Each program is arranged around a theme and use children's literature as the focus. Themes include *Courage*, *Friendship*, and *Journeys*. For more information, contact the Vermont Center for the Book or the New Hampshire Humanities Council (see *Resources*).

### Hawaii State Public Library System

Young Adult drama and discussion programs are developed by the Young Adult Services Division of the Hawaii State Library System, with funding from the Hawaii Committee for the Humanities and in cooperation with the Kapiolani Community College, the University of Hawaii, and the Friends of the Library of Hawaii. Each program includes fully costumed performers enacting scenes from literature, post-performance discussion with a scholar, and distribution of a short locally-produced reader and reading lists. Example themes are:

- *Love Triangles: Traditions of Love, Friendship, and Loyalty in American and Polynesian Culture*
- *Funny Kine: Humor and the Humanities*
- *Classic Teens: A Look at Shakespeare's Young Heroes and Heroines*
- *Gotta Match: Courtship and the Humanities*

For more information, contact Nyla Fujii or Brenda Freitas-Obregon in Program Development Services, Hawaii State Public Library System, 3255 Salt Lake Blvd., Honolulu, HI 96818. (808) 831–7896.

### Kansas Humanities Council

*Stories to Live By: Health and Medicine in Literature* is one of their reading series available for loan within the state. For information, contact Peggy Sullivan at the Council (see *Resources*).

### Let's Talk About It Delaware

Sponsored by the Delaware Library Association with funding from the NEH, Delaware Let's Talk About It has produced a number of reading and discussion themes which are shared with libraries in the Delmarva (Delaware, Maryland, Virginia) region. The most recent are:

- *And Justice for All*
- *The Chesapeake Bay*
- *Rogues' Gallery: The Folks You Love To Hate*
- *From Petitioner to Participant: Women and the Power of the Vote*

For more information, contact Truth Schiffauer (see *Resources*).

### Let's Talk About It Michigan

In 1987, to celebrate Michigan's sesquicentennial, the Library of Michigan, with funding from the Michigan Council for the Humanities, developed its own *Let's Talk About It* program. The program consists of four individual themes, each independent but interrelated through the Michigan connection, and all using Michigan authors. They are: *Mysterious Michigan, Novels Native and Near, The Michigan Experience,* and *Lines for Our Times.*

*Dynamics of Democracy* is another Michigan-produced reading and discussion program. Created by the Library of Michigan with funding from the Michigan Council for the Humanities, the Michigan Commission on the Bicentennial of the United States Constitution, and the Citizens Insurance Company of America. There are three series: *Our Constitution: The Great Balancing Act, The Constitution: Our Written Legacy,* and *Securing Our Rights: The Process of Freedom.*

The Michigan Center for the Book at the Library of Michigan also compiles a directory of humanities scholars and of Michigan libraries offering adult reading and discussion programs.

For more information, contact Joan C. Smith, Director of Special Projects (see *Resources*).

### Let's Talk About It Oklahoma

Each year since 1985, the Oklahoma Library Association has sponsored "Let's Talk About It" programs, both the national themes and locally developed ones. Usually funded by the Oklahoma Foundation for the Humanities, the program maintains a scholar directory, has produced its own planning and training guide for librarians, hires scholars to develop new themes, and produces publicity packages for each theme. Fifty libraries in Oklahoma have held "Let's Talk About It" programs each year. The library pays $50 for the publicity package and pays the postage to borrow sets of the books.

The fifteen locally developed topics include:

- *Many Trails, Many Tribes: Images of the American Indian in American Fiction*

- *The Cowboy*
- *Private Investigations: Hard-Boiled and Soft-Hearted Heroes*
- *Los Americanos Desonocidos: Contemporary Latin American Fiction*

A new theme on anthropology and literature is currently being developed by Jennifer Kidney, the project director.

For reading lists and other information, contact her at the Norman Public Library, 225 N. Webster Street, 73069. (405) 321–1481 ext. 127 or (405) 329–3395.

## Louisiana Native Grounds

A joint project of the Louisiana Library Association and the Louisiana Endowment for the Humanities, *Native Grounds: Library Reading Programs in History and Culture* includes four series:

- *The Native American World*
- *Literary Lagniappe*
- *Louisiana History*
- *Folktales and Stories of the South and Louisiana*

In addition to these Louisiana-based programs, other themes are available. Paperback books used in previous reading and discussion series are for sale at fifty percent discount. For information, contact James A. Segreto at the Endowment (see *Resources*).

## Maine State Library

*Fear and Hope: Writing from the Great Depression of the 1930s* is one of their reading and discussion series available for loan within the state. For information, contact Peggy Stewart at the Maine State Library, State House Station 64, Augusta, ME 04333. (207) 287–6250.

## Massachusetts Foundation for the Humanities

*Science As Literature* is one of their themes available for loan within the state. For information, contact the Foundation (see *Resources*).

## Metronet/Minnesota Center for the Book

The Minnesota Center for the Book develops exhibits, reading and discussion programs, listening/discussion programs, viewing/discussion programs, and performance and video programs. Most are created in-house, though Library of Congress Center for the

Book programs and Minnesota Book Awards exhibits are imported. As the statewide "focus point" for the Minnesota Study Circle Network, the Center also produces forums and promotes local study circle discussion groups.

For more information, contact Mary Treacy at Metronet, 2324 University Avenue West, Suite 116, St. Paul, MN 55114. (612) 646–0475.

## New England Foundation for the Humanities Resource Center

Originally started by six state library agencies and other library groups in New England, with funding from the NEH, the New England Foundation for the Humanities, the New England Telephone Company, and the Rhode Island Foundation, the *New England Bookbag* promoted the shared and continued use of reading and discussion programs developed in the region. Now known as the *Resource Center*, it is funded by the NEH and NYNEX and supported by the six humanities councils "to extend the life of humanities reading and discussion series."

One hundred themes originally created by state humanities councils and/or library agencies are currently available from the Resource Center which is housed at the New England Foundation for the Humanities. The topics include:

- *The Civil War: A Second Look*
- *The Other Boston Tea Party*
- *Deciding Justice*
- *Yankees and Strangers*

For more information on these themes, or to borrow multiple copies of books from these and other series, contact Renee Rubin at the Foundation (see *Resources*).

## New England Foundation for the Humanities

In addition to coordinating the Humanities Resource Center, discussed above, the New England Foundation funds the development of local discussion themes. *After Frost: Poetry in New England* is a series being presented in twenty-eight New England public libraries during 1995 and 1996. Each program consists of six group meetings to discuss thirty poets whose works have been compiled into a special reader (to be published next year by the University of Massachusetts Press). Two additional sessions feature poetry readings by visiting New England poets. The project director, Julia Walkling, reports that this is the most successful of the many programs she has developed over the past years. Another especially interesting program is *Family Scrapbooks: Films, Stories, and Conversations Looking at Different Traditions* which is a joint project of public libraries and senior centers.

For more information, contact her at 34 Boody Street, Brunswick, ME 04011. (207) 725–6353.

## New Books, New Readers (Literacy)

A project of the Maine Humanities Council, *New Books, New Readers* is based upon the successful programs in New Hampshire and Vermont. As the director, Julia Walkling, states "Participants learn to love reading when they're engaged in discussion centered on humanities themes, themes that relate to their lives." Each series uses nine children's books (reading levels grade one to grade six) on a common theme. Adult new readers participate with their tutors in three discussions led by specially trained leaders at the community library. Transportation costs and childcare are provided as necessary and participants are given copies of the books to keep.

For more information, contact Julia Walkling, at the above address.

## New Jersey Committee for the Humanities

Each year the Committee develops a reading and discussion series which are made available to libraries throughout the US. Topics include:

- *Japan: A Cultural Overview*
- *Latin American Short Stories*
- *Our Canadian Neighbors*

For information, contact the Committee (see *Resources*).

## North Carolina Center for the Book

North Carolina started *Let's Talk About It* programming in 1986 through a cooperative arrangement which still exists between the State Library of North Carolina and the Duke University Continuing Education Office. All of the ALA themes have been done in the state with fifty different libraries participating for a total of 140 series. North Carolina has also developed a number of its own statewide reading and discussion themes including:

- *Tar Heel Fiction: Literary Perspectives on North Carolina*
- *Faith Differences, Different Faiths: Exploring Religion in Modern American Fiction*

- *Mysteries: Clues to Who We Are*
- *Mysterious Fears and Ghostly Longings*
- *Science Fiction and Fantasy: Exploring Who We Are, Imagining Who We Might Become*

One hundred copies of each title from eleven *Let's Talk About It* series are available for free loan anywhere in the country (borrower pays shipping).

Other reading and discussion programs are coordinated by the Center for the Book which was created at the State Library of North Carolina in 1995. The center director, Frannie Ashburn, received a 1995–1996 grant from the NEH to produce *Poetry Spoken Then And Now: Reading and Discussion Programs in Carolina Libraries* in both North and South Carolina. She also coordinates both states' involvement with *Choices for the 21ˢᵗ Century*.

For more information, contact Frannie Ashburn at the Center for the Book (see *Resources*).

### Ohio Humanities Council

*Community Reconsidered* is the overarching theme of three discussion series:

- *Stories and Living A Life*
- *Living Together*
- *Communities At Work*

The first two are reading series, the third is a video series. For information and brochures, contact the Council (see *Resources*).

### Pennsylvania Humanities Council

Reading series include:

- *Peoples of Pennsylvania*
- *Women and Society*
- *Health and Human Values*
- *Through Women's Eyes*

The Council also coordinates the three state program *Storyline* described on p. 118. For information on any of these, contact the Council (see *Resources*).

### Prime Time Family Literacy

Children's literature (both print and audiocassette books) and story-tellers combine in humanities-based discussion programs for parents and young children. Designed to encourage the love of reading and discussing books, readings include books on world culture, history, folk tales, and fairy tales. For more information, contact the Louisiana Endowment for the Humanities (see *Resources*).

### Reading Georgia

Reading and discussion series and lecture programs are provided to libraries by the Georgia Humanities Council: *Homeplace: A Celebration of Family* and *Cultural Crisis and Compromise of Georgia's Native American Indians with the Early White Settlers.* In addition, three series on Georgia authors are available:

- *A Sense of Place: Georgia Through Time*
- *A Sense of Place: Contemporary Georgia*
- *A Celebration of Local Authors*

For information, contact the Georgia Humanities Council (see *Resources*).

### South Carolina Let's Talk About It

The South Carolina project, which shares a director with its North Carolina counterpart, has offered all of the ALA series and *Choices for the 21st Century*. It has also created its own theme *Remember Everything: The Importance of Heritage in South Carolina.* Multiple copies of the books are available for loan.

Currently, South Carolina and North Carolina are jointly doing *Poetry Spoken Then and Now*, a reading, viewing, listening, and discussion series based on *Voices and Visions* and *Poets in Person.* Co-sponsored by the NC Center for the Book, the Anderson County (SC) Public Library, and the SC Association of Public Library Administrators, the project is funded by NEH.

For information on any of the above, contact Frannie Ashburn at the Center for the Book (see *Resources*).

### South Dakota Humanities Council

The Council has developed a number of reading and discussion series for use by libraries throughout the state and elsewhere. Some themes have been:

- *Braided Lives*
- *Growing Up Chicano/Growing Up Chicana*

For information, study guides, leader packets, and posters, contact the Council (see *Resources*).

### State Historical Society of Wisconsin

*Reading the Past into the Present* is a "history reading-discussion program" developed by the historical society with funding from NEH for use in local Wisconsin public libraries. The first theme—in 1992—was *More Than Just Cowboys and Indians* about the development of the west. Participants receive three books written by historians, a specially compiled reader of essays, and a packet of supplementary materials such as transcripts of original historical documents. Since then six other themes—including *Liberty's Origins: The History of Freedom in America, The Making of the American Landscape,* and *Touched With Fire: The Impact of the Civil War*—have been created, and three are currently under development. 75 Wisconsin libraries have participated. For more information, contact Ellen Goldlust at the Society, 816 State Street, Madison, WI 53706. (608) 264-6400.

### State Library of Iowa

The State Library coordinates the use of a number of reading and discussion series, including *Poets in Person, Voices and Visions,* and *Let's Talk About It.* In addition, they have a number of locally produced themes including:

- *Images of the Future*
- *Detective Fiction*
- *Small Towns*
- *Science Fiction*

Some of these are available for loan to libraries throughout the US. For information, contact Helen Dagley, State Library of Iowa, East 12th and Grand Streets, Des Moines, IA 50319. (515) 281-3063.

### Storyline

*Storyline* is an exciting joint project of the humanities councils of Delaware, New Jersey, and Pennsylvania. Monthly book discussion programs are held on the radio with listeners calling in with their reactions to a panel of guests discussing the book. Although libraries are only minimally involved with the program (the publicity states "Book selections will be available at local bookstores and libraries . . . "), this model could be used by libraries in cooperation with their local radio stations and humanities councils. For more information, contact the Pennsylvania Humanities Council (see *Resources*).

### Vermont Center for the Book

From the Vermont Reading Project, founded in 1985 by the Vermont Library Association, grew the independent Vermont Center for the Book. Founded in 1993 to "form and foster communities of readers who use books and discussion as tools for investigating ideas and for understanding and shaping the world around them," the Center receives funding from the NEH, the National Science Foundation, the Lila Wallace-Reader's Digest Fund, and other foundations and organizations to "introduce books and informed discussion to a variety of readers."

Developed in 1995 and funded by the NEH, *A Conversation About the Search For American Identity* is now one of the Center's major programs. Twenty-eight reading and discussion programs, each focusing on four books, have been developed. For example, *Americans Rebel* includes Thoreau's *Civil Disobedience*, Chopin's *The Awakening*, Salinger's *Catcher in the Rye*, and *The Autobiography of Malcolm X*.

The Center also developed *Connections*, twelve literature-based literacy programs for adult new readers and at-risk middle and high school students. After reading books at the correct reading level for them (picture book through short novel) the new readers meet in the local library for a scholar-led group discussion on the theme. Themes include *Courage, Justice, Folktales*, and *Home*. Participants are then given the books to keep and to share with their families.

For more information on any of their programs, contact the Center (see *Resources*).

### Wisconsin Humanities Council

Series include:

- *The Storytellers*
- *Lively Listening*
- *A Sense of Place in History and Literature*

For information, contact the Committee (see *Resources*).

# MODEL LOCALLY DEVELOPED PROGRAMS

## READING AND DISCUSSION PROGRAMS

### Anderson Public Library (IN)

Six different perspectives on mysteries are included in *Murder in the Library*. For brochure (reading list), contact Anderson Public Library, 111 E. 12ᵗʰ Street, Anderson, IN 46016. (317) 641–2462.

### Anderson County Library (SC)

Women authors and their women detectives form the theme *An Unsuitable Job for a Woman*. Sets of books are available to libraries in South Carolina wishing to replicate the program. Another theme, *Memories: Recreated Visions of the Past*, incorporates film into the reading and discussion. For brochures (reading lists), contact Carl Stone, Anderson County Library, 202 E. Greenville Street, PO Box 4047, Anderson, SC 29622. (803) 260–4503.

### Baldwin Public Library (MI)

Since the onset of *Writers Live!* in 1992, the Baldwin Public Library has been a participant. In some years, the library has combined *Writers Live!* with reading and discussion programs by inviting an author being discussed or by creating discussion series based on the visiting authors' work. The library, with funding from the Friends and the Michigan Humanities Council, offers two reading and discussion series each year, both national *Let's Talk About It* series and homegrown ones. Examples of the latter are:

- *Writing One's Life: The Facts and the Fiction*
- *Booker Prize Winners*
- *Cultures in Conflict*
- *American Voices: The West*
- *American Voices: The South*

For more information contact Sarah Ormond, Head, Adult Reading Department, Baldwin Public Library, 300 W. Merrill Street, Birmingham, MI 48012–3002. (810) 647–1700.

### Brunswick-Glynn Regional Library (GA)

This library offers varied programs, including film series, lectures, author readings, and book discussions. In addition, with grant funding, more unusual and ambitious programs are designed. These are full-day programs, which combine author lectures with scholar-led public discussion. One recent topic was *Seeking the Future in the Past: Science Fiction in the South* with authors Michael Bishop, Tom Deitz, John Kessel, Ursula Le Guin, and Jack McDevitt. Others were *Writing Wrongs: True Crime Literature in the South* and *Murder They Write: Suspense, Mystery, and Mayhem in Southern Fiction*. For more information, contact Cary Knapp, Adult Services Librarian, Brunswick-Glynn Regional Library, 208 Gloucester Street, Brunswick, GA 31523–0901. (912) 267–1212.

### Buffalo and Erie County Public Library (NY)

Book Lovers of Our Metropolis (BLOOM) is the name of the planning committee for a successful ongoing cooperative venture linking book discussions with food. Eight programs a year are held at local restaurants which provide free hors d'oeuvres to participants. Many members of the audience partake of the cash bar and/or stay for dinner after the program, but no one is expected to purchase anything. The library has found that attendance far exceeds previous discussion series held in the library, and that the "Bistro Bookers" approach takes no additional staff time or expenditures. For more information, contact: Michael Mahoney, Community Relations Officer, Buffalo & Erie County Public Library, Lafayettte Square, Buffalo, NY 14203–1887. (716) 858–8900.

### Cedar Rapids Public Library (IA)

Developed by the library with a grant from the US Institute of Peace, *Israeli-Palestinian Conflict: Seeking a Common Ground* is a reading and discussion series which focuses on the individuals and families caught up in the political struggle. For information, contact Janet Rater, Cedar Rapids Public Library, 500 First Street SE, 52401. (319) 398–5123.

### Decorah Public Library (IA)

*A Thousand Acres: An Iowa Tragedy* is a reading and discussion program based on the Jane Smiley novel and Shakespeare's *King Lear* on which it was based. Copies of the two books, study guides, and a lecture text are available for loan. Contact Wanda Gardner at the library, 202 Winnebago Street, 52101. (319) 382–3717.

### Enoch Pratt Free Library (MD)

In collaboration with the city's literacy program and with funding from the Maryland Humanities Council, the city launched *Family Matters* in 1996. To encourage youth to read and discuss books on family themes, a six week reading and discussion series for teens and their parents or caregivers is being offered at two public housing sites. After a talk by a humanities scholar, librarians will lead the discussion. TV celebrities and storytellers will make appearances, and paperback copies of the books will be given to participants. For more information, contact James Welbourne, Assistant Director of The Enoch Pratt Free Library, 400 Cathedral Street, Baltimore, MD 21201 (410) 396–5484 or Barbara Sarudy, Director, Maryland Humanities Council (see *Resources*).

### Flathead County Library (MT)

A unique program, *Big Sky Radio* is a radio call-in show on Montana literature. Twelve weekly programs, each on a different book, are broadcast with audience members and scholars discussing the readings on the air via toll-free telephone. Funded by NEH and sponsored by the county library, the library provides reading lists, study guides, and books to individuals and will lend program tapes, guides, brochures, and posters to libraries. For more information, contact Flathead County Library, 247 First Avenue East, Kalispell, MT 59901. (406) 758–5820.

### Havre-Hill County Library (MT)

Four reading and discussion series have been recently developed by the Havre-Hill County Library. They are:

- *Windows on Another World*
- *Conflict/Resolution*
- *Men's Voices*
- *Family Values: Virtues and Victims*

For information and brochure or to borrow copies of available books, contact Bonnie Williamson, Havre-Hill County Library, 402 Third Street, Havre, MT 59501. (406) 265–2123.

### Howard County Library (MD)

Pat Bates, one of the founders of *Let's Talk About It* and a major proponent of the use of humanities scholars in public library-based reading and discussion, originally planned and implemented projects in Vermont. Since moving to Howard County in 1987, she has developed six NEH funded reading and discussion programs which have reached 35,000 people in Maryland. Her latest NEH-funded program includes sites in Virginia, Pennsylvania and Washington, DC. She has also produced seven other programs with funding from the Maryland Humanities Council and the US Institute of Peace. Some of her themes are:

- *Russia and Eastern Europe*
- *Winds of Change: The Middle East*
- *Morality and the Muse*
- *The 20s and 30s: Literature Mirrors History*
- *The US and the UN in the Post-Cold War World*
- *Reader, Writer, Muse*

One theme, *God, Evil, and the Literary Imagination*, was developed specifically for public libraries to use in cooperation with senior sites.

Bates often writes other libraries into her grant requests. In addition, sets of books are sometimes available to libraries wishing to replicate the programs. For brochures (reading lists) on the series listed above or for other examples, contact her. (See *Resources*).

### L.E. Phillips Memorial Public Library (WI)

In Eau Claire, Wisconsin, locally planned seminars, panels, and reading and discussion programs are offered in addition to national programs such as *Writers Live!* For more information, contact Mildred Larson, Associate Director, 400 Eau Claire Street, 54701. (715) 839–5002.

### Livonia Public Library (MI)

In cooperation with Madonna University and with funding from the Michigan Humanities Council, the Carl Sandburg Branch of the Livonia Public Library has developed a number of reading and discussion themes. The most recent are:

- *Dead White Male Writers Still Worth Reading*
- *Multifaceted Works by Multifaceted Women*
- *Historical Personalities: Real and Imagined*

For information, contact Suzanne Kys, Michigan Humanities Council, 119 Pere Marquette Drive, Suite 3B, Lansing, MI 48912–1231. (517) 372–7770.

### Loudon Public Libraries (VA)

The Loudon Public Libraries has established itself as "a vital cultural center in northern Virginia" by presenting a large array of programs of all types. The library participates in national initiatives (such as *Choices for the 21ˢᵗ Century* and *Poets in Person*) and also creates its own programs. Recent programs, funded by many sources including the Kittering Foundation, the US Institute for Peace, the Virginia Foundation for the Humanities and Public Policy, and the Lila Wallace-Reader's Digest Fund, include:

- *Archaeology, the Evidence of History: The Meeting of Indians, Europeans, and Africans in Virginia*
- *A Commonwealth of Nations: Children of Immigrants*
- *Peace and Security: Nuclear Age Concerns*
- *Mysteries of the Pyramids*

One of the more unusual programs offered was *Breaking the Sound Barrier: The Literature of Deafness* in 1993. The six part reading and discussion series was led by deaf and hard of hearing scholars and authors. Linda Holtslander, the Library Systemwide Services Manager, reports that the series was developed in response to interest shown at a focus group of people with disabilities which was convened to discuss the library building plan. Since then, the library has had many programs based on the deaf community. All programs are either sign language or voice interpreted so that all may attend.

Forthcoming programs include *Beyond Blood and Guts: Violence and Community* which is co-sponsored by the First Baptist Church, the Hand Workshop (an inner city youth art program), and the Loudon City Youth Shelter.

### Michigan City Public Library (IN)

For over ten years, the library has held a popular program *Writing Out Loud* which is an annual series of readings by "important contemporary American authors." Funded by the library and its Endowment fund, the Friends of the library, and other local sources, the programs are held primarily in the library although some have been exported to neighboring libraries and a prison. For more information, contact Kay Franklin at the library at 100 East Fourth Street, 46360–3393. (219) 873–3049.

### Middlebury Public Library (IN)

Another series on the ever-popular mystery novel, the Middlebury Public Library developed *Whodunit?* For brochure (reading list) contact the Middlebury Public Library, PO Box 192, 46540. (219) 825-5601.

### North Kingstown Free Library (RI)

For a number of years now, the library has been producing an annual scholar-led reading and discussion series with funding from the Friends of the Library. *Literary New England* focuses on poetry, short stories, novels, and films by and about New England. For more information, contact Susan Berman at the library at 100 Boone Street, 02852. (401) 294-3306.

### Oberlin Public Library (OH)

*Victims, Villains, Sleuths: The Representation of Women in Contemporary Crime Novels* is another series centering on mystery stories. For a brochure (reading list), contact the Oberlin Public Library, 65 S. Main Street, 44074. (216) 775-4790.

### Peoria Public Library (IL)

Storytelling, lectures, local and oral history, and discussion groups are all popular in Peoria, as well as the national programs *Choices for the 21ˢᵗ Century, Writers Live!* and *The Many Realms of King Arthur.* For information on their programs, contact Maggie Nelson, Peoria Public Library, 107 NE Monroe, 61602. (309) 672-8841.

### Prince George's County Memorial Library System (MD)

The Prince George's County Library produces many humanities and other programs in its nineteen branches. They have held reading and discussion series funded by the Library Foundation, the Maryland Humanities Council, the NEH, and the US Institute of Peace, and has had author programs funded by the Lila Wallace-Reader's Digest Fund. Some of their recent reading and discussion programs are:

- *American Voices*
- *America: Years of Change, 1865–1915*
- *Mad Women in the Attic*
- *In Their Own Words: Contemporary American Poets*

In March and April 1996, these other programs were offered: *Black Poets, Black Voices,* a four part reading and discussion series funded by an NEH grant to the Howard County Library; *PoetryPlus,* an ongoing poetry reading and discussion program co-sponsored by the Library Friends and a local Cultural Arts

Center; a six part lecture series on African History and Culture; the opening festivities for two exhibits: the ALA/Time Warner exhibit *It's Us: A Celebration of Who We Are in America Today* and *One More River to Cross; An African American Photo Album*; and seven author presentations (co-sponsored by a local bookstore) during National Library Week. Meanwhile, ongoing adult book discussions were held at sixteen branches and children's book discussions at three branches. A reading and discussion series is also held at a local lifecare senior residence where sixty-five residents participate regularly.

For more information, contact Judith Cooper, Development and Programming, Prince George's County Memorial Library System, 6532 Adelphi Road, Hyattsville, MD 20782. (301) 699-3500.

### Public Library of Charlotte and Mecklenburg County (NC)

Exploring the role of religion in southern fiction, *Faith and Doubt in Southern Fiction* is a four book reading and discussion series. For background notes, discussion questions, flyer, and bibliography, contact Emily McCormick, Adult Services Librarian, Public Library of Charlotte and Mecklenburg County, 310 N. Tyron Street, Charlotte, NC 28202. (704) 336-6228.

### Vienna Public Library (WV)

*West Virginia Voices* is a reading series on West Virginia Life. Series books are available for loan to WV libraries. For information, contact the Vienna Public Library, 2300 River Road, 26105. (304) 295-7771.

## READING, VIEWING, AND DISCUSSION PROGRAMS

### Anderson County Library (SC)

Films and books are used in the series *Memories: Recreated Versions of the Past*. Sets of books are available to libraries in South Carolina wishing to replicate the program. For a brochure (reading and film list), contact Carl Stone, Anderson County Library, 202 E. Greenville Street, PO Box 4047, Anderson, SC 29622. (803) 260-4503.

### Greenville County Library (SC)

Films and discussion form the programs in the five part series *Hitchcock and the Mysteries of Love*. At each session participants viewed a feature film by Hitchcock, heard a presentation by a scholar, and discussed the portrayal of men and women in the film. A recommended reading list of nine books about Hitchcock's work was developed by the scholar and distributed to participants. For a brochure (reading and film list) contact Debbie Spear, Community Services Librarian, The Greenville County Library, 300 College Street, Greenville, SC 29601-2086. (803) 242-5000, ext. 239.

### Livonia Public Library (MI)

Art, poetry, religion, social and psychological environments of Middle Eastern people are examined through print and video in *Voices From the Middle East*. For information, contact the Sandburg Branch, Livonia Public Library, 30100 W. Seven Mile, 48152. (810) 476-0700.

### Montgomery County Department of Public Libraries (MD)

Films and books are used in *Mysteries: Clues to How We Think*. For an audience guide, including bibliography and essay, contact the Montgomery County Department of Public Libraries, 99 Maryland Avenue, Rockville, MD 20850. (301) 217-3837.

### Peninsula Library System (CA)

History, ethics, and personal experiences of the Vietnam War are presented in book and videos in *Talking About Vietnam*. For a brochure (reading list), contact the Peninsula Library System, 25 Tower Road, San Mateo, CA 94402. (415) 349-5538

## READING, LISTENING, AND DISCUSSION PROGRAMS

### Monroe County Library System (MI)

A *Writers Live* participant, the Monroe County Library System hosts many types of library programs from history to computers to poetry writing. One especially exciting program is a series of lecture and demonstration programs on the blues tradition. Funded by the Michigan Humanities Council, these programs have been offered annually in observance of Black History Month for the past ten years. Different each year, the series includes musical performances, oral histories, lectures, and reading and discussion based on scholar-written booklets. Programs in 1995 covered *Women's Blues*, *The Spiritual in the Blues*, *Field to Factory*, and *Blues Individualists*. For more information, contact Tim McGorey, Community Services Coordinator, Monroe County Library System, 3700 South Custer Road, Monroe, MI 48161. (313) 241-5277.

### Redwood City Public Library (CA)

A recent series by the Redwood City Public Library, which has found its reading and discussion programs to be very popular, added listening to the mix. *The Development of the American Musical, 1865–1943*, funded by the California Council for the Humanities, used musical excerpts as well as readings. For information, contact Linda Hedges at the Redwood City Public Library, 1044 Middlefield Road, 94063–1868. (415) 780–7061.

## EXHIBITS

### Birmingham Public Library (AL)

Fifty-one hand-colored engravings of Native American culture, with descriptive text, are the focus of *Discovering America's Southeast: A Sixteenth Century View Based on the Mannerist Engravings of Theodore de Bry*. Libraries may borrow the exhibit for a fee plus round trip shipping. Catalogs are also available. For more information, contact the Birmingham Public Library, 2100 Park Place, 35203. (205) 226–3606.

### Davenport Public Library (IA)

An exhibition on Carnegie's life and philanthropy, *Andrew Carnegie and His Gifts That Continue to Grow*, is available for loan to libraries willing to pay shipping. Original brochure art is available for reproduction. For more information, contact the Davenport Public Library, 321 Main Street, 52801. (319) 326–7841.

### Newark Public Library (NJ)

Since 1990, the public library has sponsored a New Jersey Literary Heritage Conference. The 1995 symposium was on Stephen Crane and was one piece of a larger project funded by the New Jersey Council for the Humanities, the New Jersey Historical Commission, and the Friends of the Newark Public Library. In celebration of the centennial of *The Red Badge of Courage*, the library and the New Jersey Institute of Technology cosponsored a multimedia exhibit and film festival in addition to the symposium. For more information, contact the development office of the library at 5 Washington Street, 07101. (201) 733–7793.

### Newport Public Library (RI)

The library developed an exhibit entitled *China: Exploring the Interior 1903–1904* which consists of forty-nine museum quality enlargements of original photographs by R. Harvey Sargent, narrative panels, and captions. Libraries in RI may borrow it for the cost of shipping and insurance. Brochures, posters, postcards, slide sets, and bibliography are available for an extra charge.

For more information, contact the Newport Public Library, 300 Spring Street, 02840. (401) 847–8756.

### Port Washington Public Library (NY)

The library has created several exhibits which are available for loan to New York libraries only. Borrowing library pays for shipping and insurance. Poster, catalog, and curriculum guide are available for each. Examples are:

- *In the Service: Workers on the Grand Estates of Long Island, 1890s to 1940s*
- *It Looks Like Yesterday to Me: The Strength of the African American Family Over Six Generations*

For more information, contact Elly Shodell at One Library Drive, 11050. (516) 833-4400.

### Richmond Public Library (VA)

One hundred original Dick and Jane primary readers, grouped by decade, and one hundred color enlargements from the readers, are the centerpiece of the exhibit *The Story of Dick and Jane*. Libraries may borrow the exhibit for the cost of shipping and insurance. Brochure, poster, and video also available. For more information, contact the Friends of the Richmond Public Library, 2608 E. Grace Street, 23223. (804) 649–8564.

# RESOURCES: READING & DISCUSSION PROGRAMS

Deborah Robertson and Susan Brandehoff
Public Programs
American Library Association
50 E. Huron Street
Chicago, IL 60611
545–2433 ext. 5057, 5054
(312) 280–3224 (fax)

Maurvene D. Williams, Program Officer
*Center for The Book, State Centers for the Book*
Library of Congress
Washington, DC 20540
(202) 707–5221

Frannie Ashburn
*Center for the Book*
*State Library of North Carolina*
109 E. Jones Street
Raleigh, NC 27601–2807
(919) 733–2570

Sally Anderson
*Center for the Book (Vermont)*
PO Box 441
Chester, VT 05143
(802) 875–2751

Nancy Pearl
*Center for the Book*
*Seattle Public Library*
1000 Fourth Avenue
Seattle, WA 98104
(206) 386–4184

Marta Daniels
*Choices for the 21ˢᵗ Century Library Program*
Watson Institute, Box 1948
Brown University
Providence, RI 02912
(401) 863–3155

Kate Oser
*Connecticut Reading Connections*
Southern Connecticut Library Council
2405 Whitney Avenue
Hamden, CT 06501
(203) 248–6370

Sylvia Riggs Liroff
*Discovery Through the Humanities*
National Council on the Aging, Inc.
600 Maryland Avenue SW, West Wing 100
Washington, DC 20024
(202) 479–6990

Beth Bingham
*East Baton Rouge Parish Library*
7711 Goodwood Blvd.
Baton Rouge, LA 70806
(504) 389–3360

*Great Books Foundation*
35 East Wacker Drive, Suite 2300
Chicago, IL 60601–2298
(800) 222–5870

Pat Bates, Adult Program Coordinator
*Howard County Library*
6600 Cradlerock Way
Columbia, MD 21045
(410) 313–7768

Helen Cox
*Human Pursuits: The Western Humanities Concern*
350 S. 400 East, Ste. 110
Salt Lake City, UT 84111
(801) 359–9670

Deborah Robertson
*Let's Talk About It*
Public Programs
American Library Association
50 E. Huron Street
Chicago, IL 60611
(800) 545–2433 ext. 5057

Linda Holtslander
*Loudon Public Libraries*
102 Heritage Way NE, Ste 103
Leesburg, VA 22075
(703) 777–0368

Mary Treacy, Director
*Metronet*
2324 University Avenue West, Suite 116
St. Paul, MN 55114
(612) 646-0475

John Rye Kinghorn
*National Issues Forum*
100 Commons Road
Dayton, OH 45459
(800) 433–7834

Renee Rubin
*Resource Center*
New England Foundation for the Humanities
80 Boylston Street
Boston, MA 02116
(617) 482–8030

Joseph Parisi
*Poets in Person*
Modern Poetry Association
60 West Walton Street
Chicago, IL 60610
(312) 253–3703

Truth Schiffauer
112 Locust Street
Newark, DE 19711
(302) 731–9332

*Study Circles Resource Center*
Topsfield Foundation
PO Box 203
Pomfret, CT 06258
(203) 928–2616

Julia Walkling
34 Boody Street
Brunswick, ME 04011
(207) 725–6353

# RESOURCES: EXHIBITS

*ALA Traveling Exhibition Program*
Public Programs
American Library Association
50 E. Huron Street
Chicago, IL 60611
545–2433 ext. 5053,5055,5056
(312) 280–3224 (fax)

*Balch Institute for Ethnic Studies*
18 South 17th Street
Philadelphia, PA 19016
(215) 925–8090, ext. 251

*Blair-Murrah Exhibitions*
Vintage Hill Orchard
Hostetter Road
Sibley, MO 64088
(816) 249–9400, 9500
(816) 249–9300 (fax)

*Exhibit Touring Services (ETS)*
Eastern Washington University
MS-159
Cheney, WA 99004
(800) 256–1256
Http:\\visual.arts.ewu.edu/ets/ets.html

*Exhibits USA*
912 Baltimore Avenue, Suite 700
Kansas City, MO 64105–1731
(800) 473–EUSA

Giulia Adelfio
Library of Congress
*Traveling Exhibitions Program*
Washington, DC 20540
(202) 707–2153 or 5223

*Humanities Exchange, Inc.*
PO Box 1608
Largo, FL 34649
(813) 581–7328

*Schomburg Center for Research in Black Culture*
Traveling Exhibition Program
515 Malcolm X Blvd.
New York, NY 10037
(212) 491–2200

*Smithsonian Institution Traveling Exhibition Service (SITES)*
Quad 3146
MRC 706
Washington, DC 20277
(202) 357–3168

*Social Issues Resources Series (SIRS)*
Customer Services
P.O. Box 2348
Boca Raton, FL 33427–2348
800–232–7477 ext. 3

*Texas Humanities Resource Center*
Banister Place A
3809 South Second Street
Austin, TX 78704
(512) 441–0288

# 10 RESOURCES: STATE HUMANITIES COUNCILS

*Alabama Humanities Foundation*
2217 10th Court South
Birmingham, AL 35205
(205) 930–0540

*Alaska Humanities Forum*
430 West 7th Avenue, Suite 1
Anchorage, AK 99501
(907) 272–5341

*American Samoa Humanities Council*
PO Box 1935
Department of Education
Pago Pago
American Samoa 96799
(684) 633–4240

*Arizona Humanities Council*
The Ellis-Shackelford House
1242 North Central Avenue
Phoenix, AZ 85004
(602) 257–0392

*Arkansas Humanities Council*
10816 Executive Center Drive, Suite 310
Little Rock, AR 72211–4383
(501) 221–0091

*California Council for the Humanities*
312 Sutter Street, Suite 601
San Francisco, CA 94108
(415) 391–1312

*Colorado Endowment for the Humanities*
1623 Blake Street #200
Denver, CO 80202
(303) 573–7733

*Connecticut Humanities Council*
41 Lawn Avenue
Wesleyan Station
Middletown, CT 06459–0185
(203) 685-2260

*Delaware Humanities Forum*
1812 Newport Gap Pike
Wilmington, DE 19808–6179
(302) 633–1888

*D.C. Community Humanities Council*
1331 H Street #902
Washington, DC 20005
(202) 347–3350

*Florida Humanities Council*
$1514^1/_2$ East Eighth Avenue
Tampa, FL 33605–3708
(813) 272–3479

*Georgia Humanities Council*
50 Hurt Plaza, SE, Suite 440
Atlanta, GA 30303–2936
(404) 523–6220

*Guam Humanities Council*
272 West Route 8, Suite 2A
Barrigada, Guam 96913
(671) 734–1713/4

*Hawaii Committee for the Humanities*
First Hawaiian Bank Building
3599 Waialae Avenue, Room 23
Honolulu, HI 96816
(808) 732–5402

*Idaho Humanities Council*
217 West State Street
Boise, ID 83702
(208) 345–5347

*Illinois Humanities Council*
618 South Michigan Avenue, 7th floor
Chicago, IL 60605–1993
(312) 939–5212

*Indiana Humanities Council*
1500 North Delaware Street
Indianapolis, IN 46202–2419
(317) 638–1500

*Iowa Humanities Board*
Oakdale Campus N210 OH
University of Iowa
Iowa City, IA 52242
(319) 335–4153

*Kansas Humanities Council*
112 SW 6th Avenue, Suite 210
Topeka, KS 66603–3895
(913) 357–0359

*Kentucky Humanities Council*
417 Clifton Avenue
University of Kentucky
Lexington, KY 40508–3406
(606) 257–5932

*Louisiana Endowment for the Humanities*
1001 Howard Avenue, Suite 3110
New Orleans, LA 70113–2065
(504) 529–2358

*Maine Humanities Council*
371 Cumberland Avenue
PO Box 7202
Portland, ME 04112
(207) 773–5051

*Maryland Humanities Council*
601 North Howard Street
Baltimore, MD 21201
(410) 625–4834

*Massachusetts Foundation for the Humanities*
One Woodridge Street
South Hadley, MA 01075
(413) 536–1385

*Michigan Humanities Council*
119 Pere Marquette Drive, Suite 3B
Lansing, MI 48912–1231
(517) 372–7770

*Minnesota Humanities Council*
26 Exchange Street
Lower Level South
St. Paul, MN 55101–2264
(612) 224–5739

*Missouri Humanities Council*
911 Washington Avenue, Suite 215
St. Louis, MO 63101–1208
(314) 621–5850

*Montana Humanities Council*
PO Box 8306
Hellgate Station
Missoula, MT 59807
(406) 243–6022

*Nebraska Humanities Council*
Lincoln Center Building, Suite 225
215 Centennial Mall South
Lincoln, NE 68505
(402) 474–4852

*Nevada Humanities Committee*
PO Box 8209
Reno, NV 89507
(702) 784–6587

*New Hampshire Humanities Council*
19 Pillsbury Street
PO Box 2228
Concord, NH 03302–2228
(603) 224–4071

*New Jersey Committee for the Humanities*
28 West State Street, 6th floor
Trenton, NJ 08608
(609) 695–4838

*New Mexico Endowment for the Humanities*
209 Onate Hall
Albuquerque, NM 87131–1213
(505) 277–3705

*New York Council for the Humanities*
198 Broadway, 10th floor
New York, NY 10038
(212) 233–1131

*North Carolina Humanities Council*
425 Spring Garden Street
Greensboro, NC 27401
(910) 334–5325

*North Dakota Humanities Council*
1900 Broadway East, Suite 3
PO Box 2191
Bismarck, ND 58502–2191
(710) 255–3360

*Commonwealth of the Northern Marina Islands*
*Council for the Humanities*
AAA-3394, Box 10001
Saipan, MP 96950
(670) 225–4785

*Ohio Humanities Council*
695 Bryden Road
PO Box 06354
Columbus, OH 43206–0354
(614) 461–7802

*Oklahoma Foundation for the Humanities*
Festival Plaza
428 West California Street, Suite 270
Oklahoma City, OK 73102
(405) 235–0280

*Oregon Council for the Humanities*
812 Southwest Washington Street, Suite 225
Portland, OR 97205
(503) 241–0543

*Pennsylvania Humanities Council*
320 Walnut Street, Suite 305
Philadelphia, PA 19106–3892
(215) 925–1005

*Fundacion Puertorriquena de las Humanidades*
Box S-4307
Old San Juan, PR 00904
(809) 721–2087

*Rhode Island Committee for the Humanities*
60 Ship Street
Providence, RI 02903
(401) 273–2250

*South Carolina Humanities Council*
1200 Catawba Street
PO Box 5287
Columbia, SC 29250
(803) 771–8864

*South Dakota Humanities Council*
Box 7050, University Station
Brookings, SD 57007
(605) 688–6113

*Tennessee Humanities Council*
1003 18th Avenue South
Nashville, TN 37212
(615) 320–7001

*Texas Committee for the Humanities*
Banister Place A
3809 South Second Street
Austin, TX 78704–7058
(512) 440–1991

*Utah Humanities Council*
350 South 400 East, Suite 110
Salt Lake City, UT 84111–2946
(801) 531–7868

*Vermont Council on the Humanities*
Main Street, PO Box 58
Hyde Park, VT 05655–0058
(802) 888–3183

*Virgin Islands Humanities Council*
GERS Building, 3rd floor
Kronprindsens Gade
PO Box 1829
St. Thomas, VI 00803
(809) 776–4044

*Virginia Foundation for the Humanities and Public Policy*
145 Ednam Drive
Charlottesville, VA 22903–4629
(804) 924–3296

*Washington Commission for the Humanities*
615 Second Avenue, Suite 300
Seattle, WA 98104
(206) 682–1770

*West Virginia Humanities Council*
723 Kanwha Boulevard East, Suite 800
Charleston, WV 25301
(304) 346–8500

*Wisconsin Humanities Council*
802 Regent Street
Madison, WI 53715
(608) 262–0706

*Wyoming Council for the Humanities*
Box 3643 - University Station
Laramie, WY 82071–3643
(307) 766–3142

*National Endowment for the Humanities*
Division of State Programs
1100 Pennsylvania Avenue NW, Room 411
Washington, DC 20506
(202) 606–8254

# 11 RESOURCES: STATE CENTERS FOR THE BOOK

*Alaska Center for the Book*
Loussac Library
3600 Denali Street
Anchorage, AK 99503–6093
(907) 278–8838

*Arizona Center for the Book*
PO Box 34438
Phoenix, AZ 85067–4438
(602) 265–2651, ext 899

*California Center for the Book*
1225 Eighth Street, Suite 345
Sacramento, CA 95814
(916) 447–6331

*Colorado Center for the Book*
1301 Arapahoe, Suite 3
Golden, CO 80401
(303) 273–5934

*Florida Center for the Book*
Broward County Library
100 South Andrews Avenue
Fort Lauderdale, FL 33301
(305) 357–7404

*Idaho Center for the Book*
Boise State University
1910 University Drive
Boise, ID 83725
(208) 385–4373

*Illinois Center for the Book*
300 South Second Street, Room 321
Springfield, IL 62705–0728
(217) 785–4326

*Indiana Center for the Book*
Indiana State Library
140 North Senate Avenue
Indianapolis, IN 46204
(317) 232–3569

*Kansas Center for the Book*
Topeka/Shawnee County Public Library
1515 SW Tenth Avenue
Topeka, KS 66604–1374
(913) 233–2040 ext. 48

*Kentucky Center for the Book*
Department for Libraries and Archives
300 Coffee Tree Road, Box 537
Frankfort, KY 40602–0537
(502) 564–8300, ext. 315

*Louisiana Center for the Book*
760 North Third Street
PO Box 131
Baton Rouge, LA 70802–0131
(514) 342–4923

*Michigan Center for the Book*
Library of Michigan
PO Box 30007
Lansing, MI 48909
(517) 373–5700

*Minnesota Center for the Book*
Metronet
2324 University Avenue W, Suite 116
St. Paul, MN 55114
(612) 646–0475

*Missouri Center for the Book*
600 W. Main Street
PO Box 387
Jefferson City, MO 65102–0387
(314) 751–3612

*Montana Center for the Book*
Montana State Library
1515 East Sixth Avenue
CAPNO 201800
Helena, MT 59620–1800
(406) 444–3115

*Nebraska Center for the Book*
Lincoln City Libraries
136 South 14th Street
Lincoln, NE 68508
(402) 441–8516

*North Carolina Center for the Book*
State Library of North Carolina
109 East Jones Street
Raleigh, NC 27601–1807
(919) 733–8748

*North Dakota Center for the Book*
North Dakota State Library
604 East Boulevard
Bismarck, ND 58505–0800
(701) 328–1303

*Ohio Center for the Book*
The State Library of Ohio
65 South Front Street
Columbus, OH 43266
(614) 644–7061

*Oklahoma Center for the Book*
Oklahoma Department of Libraries
200 NE 18th Street
Oklahoma City, OK 73105
(405) 521–2502

*Oregon Center for the Book*
Oregon State Library
State Library Building
250 Winter Street NE
Salem, OR 97310–0640
(503) 378–2112, ext. 239

*Texas Center for the Book*
Dallas Public Library
1515 Young Street
Dallas, TX 75201
(214) 670–7808

*Vermont Center for the Book*
PO Box 441
Main Street
Chester, VT 05143
(802) 875–2751

*Virginia Center for the Book*
The Library of Virginia
11th Street at Capitol Square
Richmond, VA 23219–3491
(804) 371–6493

*Washington Center for the Book*
Seattle Public Library
1000 Fourth Avenue
Seattle, WA 98104
(206) 386–4184

*Wisconsin Center for the Book*
University of Wisconsin - Whitewater
Whitewater, WI 53190
(414) 472–1006

*Wyoming Center for the Book*
Wyoming State Library
2301 Capitol Avenue
Cheyenne, WY 82002–0060
(307) 777–5915

*State Centers for the Book*
Library of Congress
Washington, DC 20540
(202) 707–5221

# BIBLIOGRAPHY

Arendt, Hannah. *Men in Dark Times*. NY: Harcourt, 1968. Page 25.

Barber, Peggy and Linda D. Crowe. *Getting Your Grant: A How-To-Do-It Manual*. NY: Neal-Schuman, 1993.

Benedetti, Robert. "Citizenship and the Humanities." *Humanities Network* 18(1): Winter 1996: 1 and 6.

Broadus, Robert N., ed. *The Role of the Humanities in the Public Library*. Chicago: American Library Assoication, 1979.

Brown, Barbara J. *Programming for Librarians: A How-To-Do-It Manual*. NY: Neal-Schuman, 1992.

California Council for the Humanities. *Biennial Report to the People of the State of California 1992–1994*. San Francisco: CCH, 1996.

Cheney, Lynne. *Humanities in America*. Washington, DC: National Endowment for the Humanities, 1988.

Durrance, Joan C. *Let's Talk About It: National Evaluation Report*. Submitted to ALA, November 25, 1987. Unpublished.

Foundation Center. *National Guide to Funding for Libraries and Information Services*. NY: Foundation Center, 1995.

Frankel, Charles. "A Humanistic Scholar Looks at the Public Library" in Broadus, Robert N., editor. *The Role of the Humanities in the Public Library*. Chicago: ALA, 1979.

Great Books Foundation Fact Sheet. Chicago: Great Books Foundation, [1995].

Hemphill, F. Cadelle and Ronald J. Manheimer. *Discussion Group Leaders Training Guide*. Washington, DC: National Council on the Aging, Senior Centers Humanities Program, 1985.

Howarth, Shirley Reiff. *Guide to Traveling Exhibition Organizers*. Fargo, FL: The Humanities Exchange, 1994.

Hurd, Patricia and Jordy Vantresca. "Poetry in the Heart of It All: The Poets in Person Series in Ohio." *Ohio Libraries* 7(3): 6–10, Summer 1994.

Lapsley, Andrea. Speech. American Library Association Midwinter Meeting (January 21, 1996: San Antonio, Texas).

Lewis, Richard A. *Discussing the Humanities.* Madison, WI: University of Wisconsin-Extension, 1974.

Martin, Patricia. Speech. American Library Association Annual Conference (June 25, 1996: Chicago).

Monroe, Margaret E. "The Cultural Role of the Public Library" in Harris, Michael H. , editor. *Advances in Librarianship.* Volume 11. New York: Academic Press, 1981.

Monroe, Margaret E. *Library Adult Education: the Biography of an Idea.* NY: Scarecrow Press, 1963.

Moores, Alan and Rhea Joyce Rubin. *Let's Talk About It: A Planner's Manual.* Chicago: American Library Association, 1984.

National Cultural Alliance. *The Importance of the Arts and Humanities to American Society: A Nationwide Survey of the American Public Commissioned by the National Cultural Alliance and Conducted by Research & Forecasts, Inc.* NY: The Alliance, 1993.

National Endowment for the Humanities. *A National Conversation: The Conversation Kit.* Washington, DC: NEH, 1994.

National Endowment for the Humanities. *Overview of Programs 1995.* Washington, DC: NEH, 1995.

National Endowment for the Humanities, Division of Public Programs. *Guidelines and Application Instructions* (draft). Washington, DC, NEH, 1996.

National Endowment for the Humanities, Division of Public Programs. *Humanities Projects in Libraries and Archives: Guidelines and Application Instructions.* Washington DC, NEH, 1994.

New England Foundation for the Humanities Resource Center. *Coordinator's Guide for Reading and Discussion Programs.* Boston: NEFHRC, 1995.

Phelps, Thomas. Correspondence with Rhea Joyce Rubin. 1995–1996.

Quay, James and James Veninga. *Making Connections: The Humanities, Culture and Community.* Washington, DC: American Council of Learned Societies (Occasional Paper No. 11), 1990.

Rader, Barbara A. "Humanities Programming in Libraries: The Connecticut Perspective." *Public Libraries* 29 (6):342–348, November/December 1990.

Rubin, Rhea Joyce. *Intergenerational Programming in Libraries: A How-To-Do-It Manual.* NY: Neal-Schuman, 1993.

Rubin, Rhea Joyce and Joan M. Durrance. "Let's Talk About It: Lessons in Adult Humanities Programming." *Public Libraries* 28(2): 90–96, Mar/Apr 1989.

Shaevel, Evelyn and Peggy O'Donnell. *Courtly Love in the Shopping Mall: Humanities Programming for Young Adults.* Chicago: American Library Association, 1991.

Study Circles Resource Center. *The Study Circle Handbook.* Pomfret, CT: Topsfield Foundation, 1993.

Taft Group. *The Big Book of Library Grant Money 1996–1997: Profiles of 1471 Private and Corporate Foundations and Direct Corporate Givers Receptive to Library Proposals.* Chicago: American Library Association, 1996.

Tuchman, Barbara. *Books in Our Future: A Report from the Librarian of Congress to the Congress.* Washington, DC, 1984. Page 1. Reprinted from "Books are the Carriers of Civilization." *Authors' League Bulletin*, December 1979.

# INDEX*

*Note: Entries that are italicized are titles of specific programs.*

# COLOPHON

Rhea Joyce Rubin is an independent library consultant, specializing in extending public library services to non-traditional users. She received both her BA and MLS from the University of Wisconsin-Madison where she studied with Margaret E. Monroe.

Active in humanities programming efforts since 1975 when she acted as a Field Director for the NEH-funded "Discovery Through the Humanities" project of NCOA, Rubin has been a trainer and evaluator for the national "Let's Talk About It" program, the coordinator for "Talking About Vietnam" and "Columbus and After," a trainer for "Poets in Person," and a panel for various other humanities projects.

Recipient of the 1993 Exceptional Service Award from ASCLA, the 1992 Margaret E. Monroe Award from RASD, and the 1980 Ralph Shaw Award from ALA, Rubin does consulting, training, project management, and writing from her base in Oakland, California.